THE SHAWCROSS LETTERS

MY JOURNEY INTO THE MIND OF EVIL

JOHN PAUL FAY
BRIAN WHITNEY

WILDBLUE
PRESS

WildBluePress.com

THE SHAWCROSS LETTERS published by:

WILDBLUE PRESS
P.O. Box 102440
Denver, Colorado 80250

Interior Formatting/Book Cover Design by Elijah Toten
www.totencreative.com

THE
SHAWCROSS
LETTERS

MY JOURNEY INTO
THE MIND OF EVIL

TABLE OF CONTENTS

Introduction   7

Chapter One   15

Chapter Two   26

Chapter Three   52

Chapter Four   63

Chapter Five   100

Chapter Six   125

Chapter Seven   140

Chapter Eight   161

Chapter Nine   173

Chapter Ten   198

Chapter Eleven   230

AFTERWORD   242

INTRODUCTION

What you are about to read is, in part, the story of Arthur Shawcross, one of the world's most prolific and brutal serial killers, told by himself through his own letters to his friend, John Paul Fay. Shawcross, who is also known as "The Genesee River Killer," was officially found responsible for the murders of twelve women in upstate New York from 1988 to 1990. His own words in this book insinuate that he may have been responsible for more killings that that. This series of murders was not the first time that he killed. In 1972, he confessed to the sexual assault and murders of two children. Shawcross is also known to have dabbled in cannibalism. This book is not the story of the crimes committed by Shawcross, nor is it a history of his life. Instead, it offers an extremely rare glimpse into the mind of a sadistic killer.

This book is also the story of John Paul Fay. John is a rather interesting man, a small-time dealer in murderabilia, a collector of shrunken heads, and the would-be biographer of Shawcross. Mr. Fay is an incredibly talented writer and a very brave one as well. He is also afflicted with many of the same types of urges and fantasies that led Shawcross to become a brutal murderer.

Why do some among us have thoughts involving ideas and fantasies that are so harmful to themselves and society? And then, why do some people act on those fantasies without remorse while others keep them locked inside forever? While Shawcross was a serial killer, Fay never killed anyone. If he had, this would be a much different book.

I probably don't have to tell you at this point that this book will be difficult to read for some. The thoughts that both

Shawcross and Fay put forth in this book will be extremely distasteful, in varying degrees, to many. While many books of this ilk are sort of in the "I became friends with a serial killer and it was so bizarre" category, what makes this unique is that Fay's story is more of the "I became friends with a serial killer and it sure was nice to finally be able to be myself around someone" type.

This book will make you uncomfortable and it will make you angry, and possibly even a bit afraid. It will also make you think. It is easy to be frightened of those around us who have dark and deviant thoughts, it is much more difficult to meet these people head on, look them in the eye, and try to understand them. There is much more light in the world than darkness, but still, darkness is all around us. Pretending it doesn't exist simply does not work.

We as a society live in fear of those around us, like Shawcross, who could hurt us, and well we should, but what of the people that are still salvageable, those that have deviant fantasies, but haven't crossed the line? Do we cast them out because they are "different" or "sick," or do we try and reach out to them and try to understand them and offer them kindness? If someone had done this with Shawcross many years ago, would he have still committed his brutal crimes? It is important as one reads this book to remember that Shawcross was an awful person, who murdered numerous people, destroyed families, and terrified communities. This book is not meant to glorify his actions nor disrespect anyone he has hurt in any way, either directly or indirectly.

What this book is meant to do is to give you a look into the mind of a serial killer who did some incredibly horrible things. It is also a rare opportunity to hear, concurrently, from someone who has desired to do similar things, but has chosen not to.

It is important to note that the letters of Shawcross have not been edited. Some of his letters are dated by him, some are not. Words that he spells incorrectly have not been changed. He goes through lists of victims in more than one letter. At times things he writes are confusing. All of this has been left intact to preserve authenticity, as it is important for the reader to know that all of the content of his letters is exactly how he wrote it.

Speaking of authenticity, Shawcross wrote two letters to Fay that are printed in this book where he falsely claimed to have written certain poems. One of these he called *Twisted*, which in reality is a common nonsense poem of unknown origin, the other he called *Love* which in actuality is 1 Corinthians 13: 4-7 from the Bible. And what of John Paul Fay? Why would he write a book of this nature? Well, in part, it is because he wants to make money to buy shrunken heads, but there are much deeper reasons, ones that he can speak to much better than I ever could.

Of this, Fay writes:

Whether it's a mysterious malady of my synapses or a misalignment somewhere in my soul, then I will take the exposure and try to be the voice of our breed whom I affectionately refer to as the Strangelings. Glorifying, romanticizing, or encouraging any of the madness is not the intention herein. Rather it is to use this medium as a kind of literary exorcism. Just a love letter of support to let the afflicted know that they are not alone. Obviously, the social repercussions of discussing these things without an especially selective screening process could be irreparably devastating. Someone, however, should speak for the exotically deranged, the men and women of aberration.

Because really, your wife would rather not hear about how lovely you think her head would look on your nightstand. Nor would your best friend titter joyously over how "wonderful" you note it might be having his mummified hands as bookends for your collection of vintage porn. Difficult propositions in polite society, and borderline illegal, perhaps. And indeed, best of luck with the mental health teams folding in on themselves and going into withdrawals if they don't have you committed by breakfast.

First rule for living insane: Do not give them an excuse! Come up with more self-constructive ways of dealing with these...challenges. Restraining orders, jails, psych wards, four and five-point restraints, continuous Section 12 & 35 commitments, and rumors of commitments and social isolation. Frustration that feels like meth-amped carpenter ants under your skin; frantically scraping caked blood off your face (originating from who knows where) on the morning of a court appearance eventually loses its luster. Eventually, but not immediately.

Of course, my own policy is "SEE NOTHING, SAY NOTHING," but this addressing of the affliction is an unusual exception. For one, I've specifically designed my life so that I'm not bothered by the concerns it seems to me everyone else is, such as standard family lives, friends, career, a fully-realized conscience, and, well, sleep; and two, using this tact, as a writer and reporter from the sludge, means I have certain license whereby the unusual will be expected of me. Aside from that, I'm in a uniquely strange position to have bonded with a hellion something-or-other that, with the routine lust of demons, basically consumed me. Indeed, I, both the Venus Fly Trap and the fly.

Whether it's a hex--or even, in some sense, a virtue--I'll take whatever socially damaging hits that may come to be a kind of inside out spokesperson for the derailed, deranged, despicable, disregarded, and discontent. But if this is damnation--if all of us are well within the borders of Hell, biding our time until our judgment (or stray-shot chance beneficence) --we're probably collectively screwed anyway. Still, it's helpful to know you're not appallingly alone. I'll be here, dead or alive.

Enjoy the book.

A Dedication of Eternal Gratitude: For the angels of tattered wings and wicked things.

The ones who brokered "the Deal." --JPF

CHAPTER ONE

When God died, the world went berserk.

As a directly connected note and, perhaps, a warning before proceeding, the almost familial relationship I had with Arthur Shawcross, one of history's most terrifying serial killers and admitted (often, boastfully so) cannibals, was a decidedly unholy one.

My relationship to Arthur Shawcross was the closest to a wholesome relationship I've yet had. It has continued to be so. Of course, let it be noted, "wholesome" is a relative designation, as I don't abide the concept of human relationships the way an average individual does.

Not only did I swan dive into the rabbit wormhole, I demolished the only way in or out. Through either willful incompetence, or concentrated free will and accord, to open a vein to attempt an under-the-radar flight from the profanity of a monochrome existence, I made it a preposterous impossibility to reverse course. Whatever, I'm here now, just swinging at the ball as it comes.

The grit.

The grime, the slime, the crime, and the grim, seductive sublime.

The night-washed alleys and sleepily-lit hallways where the dreary, weary, and shady ride out a nod, disguised by their own layer cakes of filth, one get-well-soon spike or dope-sick robbery from overdose or a life sentence.

The backrooms, basements, bunkers, and burnout bachelor pads quietly hiding odd little men who own one too many axes. The secret places unobtrusively blending into the background just out of sight, out of mind.

This is where I live; this is what I live for.

I was playing peek-a-boo with the Devil long before I began my tumbles, fumbles, and stumbles through the brambles of Wonderland and the eerily precarious shores of the abyss led me to Shawcross. Or, perhaps Shawcross, the proudly self-appointed "mutant," was led to me. After all, he reached out to me first.

I'm not entirely certain what this says about my character, but I could never have dreamed how important a figure, at a deeply personal level, Arthur Shawcross was about to become for me. It went well beyond our business arrangements and book agreement. I became dependent on his presence to validate my own minefield of a mind, which was already uniquely primed and wired as unspecified bipolar with antisocial traits. According to a myriad of rather unfortunate psychiatrists I have seen, I am also afflicted with PTSD, OCD, and, occasionally, a psychotic episode to keep people around me on their toes.

There's no denying that inside of me, as my own descent into a Hell-spun lunacy was just getting underway, Shawcross grew roots, integrating into my life as a surreal, symbiotic, perversion of the surrogate father-son dynamic.

Shawcross was the quintessential enabler, a recurring echo goading me into more and more misadventurous indulgences of my tendencies for exorbitantly bizarre behaviors, an ever-present voice interwoven into the hallucinatory soundtrack of my life, founded on the fallen, twisted trees of a ceaselessly treacherous forest.

One or two sharp, brief breaths of counsel here. Don't play with black magic, demons, or, indeed, the Devil Himself, unless you want what you're calling. In other words, do be careful what you wish for. Be dedicated or just be dead. And if you're insane, don't take said insanity lightly. Though, it can, and does, keep life engaging.

Whether ritual magic brings madness or madness leads one to find such things appealing in the first place, I couldn't aptly uncover. In either case, I have my suspicions that Shawcross might have been the ultimate embodiment of my blindly pursuing the darkest of occult sciences, arts, and necromancy, dredging devils from the Pit just to keep me company.

The same reason that I chose, in my drunken hazes, to keep certain friends around for longer than maybe they'd intended. Although the law calls it "false imprisonment," it was real enough for all involved. Certain key details might not be recalled entirely due to chronic alcoholic blackouts, but some graciously administered prescription sleeping medication somehow being mixed into drinks and guests coming out of deep, deep rest the next day or two later, shackled to their bed, may possibly have been an odd phase I went through. No allegations have been made, so this might all be strange delusion. What I can recount clearly was that I was a captive of myself as well, cuffing and shackling my own hands and feet many times over, long before my actual arrests, to get acclimated to moving about with such restrictions. A self-fulfilling prophecy, I suppose. Certainly, I didn't help it not to happen.

When I was ten, my parents pulled their worst off-balancing act up to that point, separated and shuffled their children to any family members who would take us out of pity more than graciousness, establishing us as what my maternal grandmother called "latchkey kids." I felt lost, needing connection to something, someone, anything, anyone. Auntie Lorraine, my father's sister who assumed the role of unofficial surrogate mother, used to take me out for daytrips into witch territory Salem and occasionally treated me to lunch with the witches (I met world-renowned witch Laurie Cabot once at one of those lunches and she very respectfully advised me on a dream potion I'd wanted to try), palm and tarot card readings, life-altering Ouija board sessions, and bought me an elaborate library of books on occult magic and Satanic sciences. My intrigue with the practice of magic took hold of me the way that hard drugs would later. For certain, it was addicting, but it kept a lonely boy busy. My occupation was self-destruction right from the beginning.

Digesting each book, I was especially drawn to the revelation that one could call entities over from wherever they resided. In my reeling desolation, with such an emotionally confused barrier between myself and most everyone else, I thought of it as a friend-on-demand (or more realistically, demon-on-demand). It was hope for something different, something better. My life from the beginning had been a daily carpet bombing of behind-closed-doors abuse and dread, so there really wasn't much to lose.

Experimenting with spells seemed like something over which I could have relative control. It was only the clueless summoning of a randomly chosen demon from a book of black magic incantations, invocations, evocations, provocations, irritations, and optional mutilations. The book was a no-special-occasion gift from Auntie Lorraine, who my parents took full advantage of as far as dumping their children onto, as my "mother" had only had her three children for cosmetic purposes, a sick façade of normalcy, and a pathological need for attention. In the moment, as a child playing with devils beckoning just where Earth and Hell converged, while other children wrapped themselves up in what I considered the most mundane and bloodless of activities, I thought I'd not performed the ritual correctly, or that it simply didn't work.

Much later, I agonized over whether I engaged in an invocation rather than an evocation, or some magical mash-up symbiosis of spells. The summation of said summoning, an invocation is inviting a spirit or demon/jinn into yourself, an evocation is calling these forces outside of yourself at a relatively safe distance. Decades later, emptying bottle after bottle of rum, chasing nearly every mind-altering alchemical substance known to humankind, I wondered if maybe I had not failed at summoning something after all. Particularly, on cocaine I tend to do a lot of wondering aloud. And, may the late-to-the-party Lord help me, I have a racecar-in-the-red proclivity for other radically morbid musings of possibly interdimensional proportions. But it doesn't become overtly dangerous until I remember where I hid the knives. Of course, crazy saves me.

My curiosity came from a deadly serious place. It wasn't only the possibility of having brought an incarnate demon, in the form of Arthur Shawcross, into my life, but some intangible, churning fog rolling with a speed of driven determination, of the most exotic tint of the macabre into myself.

For the uninitiated, the otherwise profane, and those not well rooted to the Underbelly--where even the air is not for the faint of heart: when the wolves are at your door, it's best not to answer. You can't tease demons, who command full-bore commitment. The Devil won't slip a ring around your finger but around your neck. And these forces from well over the rainbow will drag you through the mud like a dumbfounded dog if you're not mindful and always respectful. Candidly speaking then, DO NOT do what I did. Not only did I answer the door, I invited the Beast in with the morbid giddiness of some mad occult scientist. Though, this seemed to be my nature anyway, however unnatural it may be.

Looking back now, that first piece of mail from the Sullivan Correctional Facility was a slow-motion spark heading into a sea of gasoline and dynamite.

6-25-00

Mr. John Fay,

Are you by any chance known by the handle, SAWMAN?

Sometimes I examine who is who on the market. I've quite a list of buyers and sellers. The sellers I stop writing to! That is if the sell my letters to others!

I am leery of who I write to in the mail.

Do you know a Melissa from Ripon, CA? I've a few photos of her. I can say MUCH on that one.

Let's talk for a while truthful to each other.

A.J.S.

Another rule to pay mind to: NEVER take a human skull to a job interview with you. That being noted, it was during the "Golden Age" of eBay. For me at least, but I was bootlegging every imaginable genre of film and auctioning sideshow curios and gaffs including the perennially popular shrunken heads, back when any perfectly sane enterprising capitalist could auction the artifacts of murderers (aka Murderabilia).

For someone like me, who was not all that employable, mainly because of my penchant for trying to strangle bosses, this was a respectable supplemental income. I managed to get my hands on several pieces of Shawcross's artwork (some meticulous 8" x 10" pencil drawings of birds) in a quite amusing trade with a fellow eBayer. She was a female fan of Shawcross and other serial killers throughout the country. I'd traded her a number of homemade video compilations of serial killer interviews, documentaries, and news footage, which I had put together. This kind of subject matter is, as I empirically observed, far more popular than a society of people wearing masks of normalcy might want to know, admit, or admit to knowing.

Financially, it was sensible and sound to auction the drawings of Shawcross' blue jays, cardinals, and seagulls in flight. I figured I would just wait and see whose attention might be piqued, confident that there were other collectors into these unusual acquisitions; people whom let their personas down in the privacy of their hideaways from the world as they tentatively trawled the depths for brushes with evil at a safe distance.

That strange day in June of 2000, when I discovered the unexpected letter from Arthur Shawcross, was, as usual, a grindingly lonely one. Living alongside a shattered and scattered family, it made no difference. We were never on eye-to-eye terms and it's still impossible to imagine how I share blood with such a deranged example of humanity. Taken completely by surprise, after hesitating for half an hour or thereabouts before opening the mail, I had the distinctly alarming feeling that I might be in some kind of trouble. Like the time I was apprehended shoplifting, finally, at one of the nearby malls when I was fifteen. Wrestling ferociously with five security guards, I was eventually half carried and dragged into the department store's tight quarters of a security room. I'd been sloppy that day.

This began with the first mistake of taking my cousin Raymond instead of my usual partner-in-grime Mike, which makes for really bad luck. Apparently, it poisons the dynamic to break that connection. That had been the first apprehension I had the pleasure to experience. What this store essentially did was to extort me for two-hundred-fifty dollars rather than prosecute. So, my first actual arrest wouldn't happen for another twenty-one years, despite many police detainments, interactions, and escorts with ambulances to one hospital or another. With any situation such as this, though, one has an uneasy sense of having the cloak torn off and suddenly realizing how visible you actually are.

As for Shawcross, I worried that I hit an unfortunate nerve with this convicted serial killing cannibal. I also was moderately apprehensive about his having my home address.

A year or two later, chances are I would've taken a

blackout cocktail before reading the ice-breaking letter. As it was, I was sober as a judge is supposed to be in most modern American courtrooms, my mind sparking with apprehension, excitement, and, curiously enough, the faint hope that I'd found a new friend off the beaten path.

My policy being to keep as much to myself as was possible, I said nothing about the letter to anybody. It was none of their business. As my divorced parents, who, through some abortion of logic, were still residing in the same ass-backward household, going about their daily scenarios of monotony (my dad continued to stalk my mother even after their divorce, despite sharing the same house), and my two younger sisters impetuously pursued their strapped-for-intelligence boy toys of the month, I went ahead and opened the note. Peeling the envelope, there was a sudden concussive shock that slammed my senses. It was like some innate understanding that I had just then broken the seal on a portal into a deathly pale landscape which should not have been breached and certainly never explored. It was an expression of destiny as tailored in Hell, rising ominously as a duo of the damned and doomed.

Something I have stringently kept to myself was that my usually deadened instinct for brotherhood was buoyed to the surface by Shawcross. It was validation from the pinnacle of we, the soldiers of the macabre; a stamp of approval by one of the world's most unrepentant cannibal compatriots. Could I really have shared that with anyone of sepia-tone sensibilities with the vapid values of a plate of bacon and eggs? Dr. D, my psychiatrist, was already itching to bury me even before things really got out of control. She was a quirky doctor of psychiatry indeed, a straitjacket framed above her desk.

Not that I hadn't recognized it as an especially delicate situation. After all, I was dealing with an openly evil man whose skeletons were so out of the closet that they were re-inventing the cemetery business, handed down a two-hundred-fifty-year bid for a pastime I'd only been experiencing as phantasms, internally toying with for eight or so years at the time, as astounding and frightening in its implications as that is. What mostly concerned me was the prospect of Shawcross being unreasonably challenging. All the other male figures and ass-sideways "role models" in my shit-com of a life certainly were. Exceedingly brutal and mean-spirited men, every one of them. Of course, Shawcross wouldn't be entirely different with his own brand of brutality and intolerance, even toward me on occasion (especially near the end). But we had something in common that I characterize as the "affliction."

How in the arcane name of the devil-headed god Jahbulon of Babylon would I, or could I, respond? Play our words backwards and you'll understand that grim minds think alike, no matter what we try to say in the mundane world to diminish who we really are. I realized later that I only worried because of that often-crippling lack of self-confidence that stays on me like a perpetually wet blanket, sewn to my soul and not quite locking on to who and what I actually am. I believe that I was groomed for this sinister season, which has really been the only thing in my life I've carried a passion for that was never exhausting to me. The only thing that doesn't feel like work to love. After all, lovers quite literally come and go, whether through boredom or death, but the pursuit of subterfuge sin just doesn't seem to grow old. And it certainly won't die.

I became increasingly indignant as I processed the letter's contents, and lamented that even a habitually murdering maniac wasn't quite catching onto the gist of where I was coming from. A horrible and horrific disconnect, I felt. I did realize how careful I had to be and not write back with a psychotic's abandon. My rants have ruined me for long-term friendships before. So then, I took the path of indignation but ever so delicately. The intentions were to clear up what I believed was a misalignment of communication. If I wanted anyone to understand me, it was Arthur Shawcross. The two of us were companion madmen of the Outskirts; a netherworld director's cut of society, which I had no inclinations of departing anytime soon. As Shawcross had crossed precipices I had yet to, there was something morbidly spellbinding about him. Dare I admit, it felt like an almost inside-out romance. We weren't necessarily on the same page and wouldn't always agree on everything, or ever have perfectly matching personalities, but we were at least on the same bookshelf. An odd camaraderie, I'm the first to confess. These psychedelic shades of gray were never an easy topic to cover with the uninitiated. Not that I wish it on anyone; it skins the spirit bare.

At the beginning of it all, I pitched Shawcross a business arrangement. If he were amenable, wonderful! If not, I'd either get a response spattered with a serial killing cannibal's strain of hate or just never hear from the Genesee River Killer again. Either way, I was a battered lifetime veteran of bad starts and unhappy endings, so what would be the loss? Still, there was hope, muddied and bloodied as it was.

7/6/00

MR. FAY,

What was the drawing of mine that you sold? What did you sell the item for? I can use a money order -- only if it does not put you out! May I ask who bought said item? Can you send addresses of people who are collectors?

Where might you be moving to? Now that you have parted with one item of mine, here are two more to help you on your way, Mr. Sawman. Some handle you have there! It was the handle, Sawman, that got my attention.

I have used a MACHETE on a few...Head come right

off! Vietnam will do that to you!

Mr. Fay, I hear about letters being sold all the time. The people who do that I generally leave alone. I dislike writing to someone and have them sell a letter because I have said things that are not cool for the eyes of others!

Wish I was in Boston again. Last time I was there. I was a teenager.

Melissa of California, I'd like to rattle her bones a few times for real... she would not be the same afterward. HAHA

Mr. Fay, you now have her photos. Do as you wish with them.

Stay cool.

Later,

Arthur S.

CHAPTER TWO

DEATH BUBBLES OVER

My emotional baseline, to which I was in agreement with the program coordinator of the court-stipulated intensive outpatient program for addiction and other outlandish mental disorders, was "depressed, miserable, and unusually dark." Schizotypal was among the designated diagnoses that the coordinator gave me, gleaned from the revered DSM-5. Still it was only one facet. Whatever this thing is, it rides hard under the façade. Suffice to state, it doesn't take much to push me past my limits, maybe only an unfortunately timed nudge. However, some of the criteria does have to be taken with a grain of salt. The mental health field tends to overlook anything of a spiritual nature when it comes to diagnosing someone of my ilk, except to classify anyone adhering to such uncanny ideas as being a delusional, magical-thinking psychotic voted "Most Likely to Butcher Every Living Thing."

I did manage to roll past the initial mental tumult and torment of feeling that I'd somehow been slighted by Shawcross, coming up with an approach that might be my entree into ingratiating myself and getting on my fellow cannibal's "good side," whatever that translated to. For fuck's sake, everyone else in my life had a gross deficit in their interpretations of my personality and a line does have to be drawn somewhere. If only I could make Shawcross aware of my own monster, it might be the start of…something. I wasn't just an opportunist, civilian auctioneer exploiting everything and everyone I could for some bottom-of-the-barrel monetary scrapings. Come on, I'm practically one of you! Still, I knew that it would be in my best interests to go about this with a fragile sensibility, as I also didn't care to spook or turn him off. First, I needed to smooth things over. Then I'd go from there, to wherever that express elevator down led. As with anything else, it was a process of increments. And besides, I couldn't pencil in a war with a serial killer into my already erratic schedule of trying to figure out how to sleep on jobs where the neurotic, nitpicking bosses had the abhorrent expectations for me to go a full eight hours without a nap.

Agitated at first, I was on the verge of writing, "Dear Mr. Shawcross, How is my favorite lunatic today?" Instead, I opted to soldier on and painstakingly crafted my reply with obsessive neurosis to make literally every syllable as near to perfect as possible. I was sincere in the expression of my disappointment in Shawcross, his believing that I might cheat him. That just wasn't me. I hustled corporations, not people. Considering it reasonably pragmatic and diplomatic enough, I appealed to the universal love of money. I began pitching my unconventional acquaintance and possible acquisition what might be a financially sound proposal, which was that Shawcross could finagle some more drawings and we could then do a 50/50 split on the auctions' proceeds. It was the shot of a starter pistol to what happens when a pair of cartoonish, cataclysmic characters of undetermined origins crosses paths and never quite leaves each other's side again.

By his second letter, Shawcross seemed to have relaxed, evidently realizing that I wasn't a threat to him, and I noticed that he was gradually less formal. The first letter, signed "A.J.S.," the second "Arthur S.," and by the third, we'd made it to "Art." And he wasn't treating me as a trespassing pirate anymore, which was a real relief. Whatever I'd written had evidently worked. I was so miserably tired of alienating people, for one reason on top of another, that I made the conscious decision to nurture this relationship. My mother you could throw off the Empire State Building, but this was meaningful to me. Besides, it helped that Shawcross never openly regretted my birth as my mother had. Then again, I do welcome doom.

Further endearing him to me, he was my number one fan (even if in a Stephen King's "Misery" context) of the handle I'd used early in my eBay dealings: **Sawman.**

This was an organic choice based on a curious obsession for collecting, appropriately enough, saws of all kinds from throughout history. Aside from that, I'm a birth-to-death aficionado of horror and slasher movies, which I affectionately think of as "Gore Porn."

Once, when nineteen or twenty-years-old, I was moved to purchase eight saws and several random blades at a local "mom & pop" hardware store for no real-world application except to flirt with the fantasies. Normally, I have a just-in-case story prepared if certain inquiries arise for anything that I'm doing which might be seen as out of the ordinary or just plain old fucking weeeeeird, but, immersed in the seducing glow that reoccurs with these afflictions, not this time. It quickly became apparent that the young man tending to the register was either trying to scrape together a conversation with me or deciding whether he should make the on-the-spot decision to call the police. No way to be sure really. I was all blank when the clerk asked what I was to do with "all those saws." It wasn't my best performance, as I mindlessly stammered on about some vague job my uncle was assigning me, a model cowboy town or something, which Uncle Jerry actually did build on occasion when he got bored with drunk-punching holes in the walls or stomping rats to death with his Old West-style cowboy boots.

I know that none of this would necessarily help my cause in something like a child custody battle, even getting a date to produce the child in the first place, or running for any ostensibly respectable political office. Though, that's the reason I never had children and, to be honest, turn a blind eye to politics. Therefore, freeing me up to take on insanely self-destructive projects such as writing this personal vivisection of a book. Well, perhaps, self-destructive and a little self-loathing but not quite as self-incriminating. Certainly, I have barreled over the edge, rented out, and then finally sold my soul in other ways than Shawcross ended up doing. But, odd as it is even to me, I do have, at least according to probation officers and court records, those technically deemed as "victims". The "victim" count, by the way, seems to go plural very quickly when you're on a roll and out of control. These people are, to my knowledge, alive (or, at least, they were when I last saw them), and each official case has been sorted out legally. Although the fact that my dresser drawer is now so crammed, as it has been for the last few years, with restraining and abuse prevention orders that I practically have to use a battering ram to close it may be disconcerting for some. But what miracle worker can please everyone (or even anyone)?

Hi John:

What's doing out your way? Over here in this camp I am cold! I spent the day in my room trying to keep warm under the covers. I did go out in the rec room for an hour to speak to someone who is about to leave here for another place. He gave me some of his clothes. SIZE 3X LARGE, A brand new zippered sweater with hood, two sweatshirts that are like new and one HUGE TOWEL that I can use to wrap myself up in on the way to the shower. This man has been down 32 years! He is 67 years of age and stands 6' 4" tall. He used to be a doctor way back when before he had been arrested for shooting his unfaithful wife of eleven months! In most any other country, he might have got off. But in America he got 32 years to life!

In a Muslim country he would have spent no time in jail or prison!!!! Over there they don't hold with a woman cheating on her husband! My co-worker is pissed at me for getting all his stuff. I don't see why not as this guy does not know him at all except to say hi, that is all. This man is connected with art dealers on the outside, so I may expect someone to contact me in the next year. I hope so.

I have your letter somewhere in here but had misplaced it somehow. So I will tap one out without it in front of me. The ribbon in this machine I re-inked. Now it runs along quite well for me. I got a few Christmas cards in but these are the ones a man sends to a woman. Sorry, John, you can't get one. hahahaha One of the rich men in here gave me a cigar that is worth $6.50 each! This guy is a millionaire many times over. I invited him to have Thanksgiving with us. He was very thankful for that as no one else did! But this guy didn't put any effort into getting in anything either! Cheap in a way! He left yesterday for the streets. I may or may not hear from him again. Who can say? I take a person at his word and if he says he will do something for me I expect him to do it and come back with no bullshit! Some guys I don't put much thought into. One man just came in two days before Thanksgiving and I asked him to eat with us. He was very thankful. He knew my name anyway. He said every inmate up North knows who I am. Must be nice to be famous--or is it INFAMOUS? Whichever… What gets me is that I hear from people who tell me they hear about my cooking way up there! It seems that word of mouth travels fast in the system! I can say that I prepared a feast for Thanksgiving Day evening.

My menu for this year: HONEY-ROASTED CHICKENS, MASHED POTATOES, STUFFING, SWEET POTATOES, SWEET PEAS, MIXED VEGETABLES, CRANBERRY SAUCE AND BERRIES, RICE WITH OCTOPUS & SHRIMP, RICE WITH BLACK BEANS AND PEPPERS, RICE W/BLACK EYE PEAS/HOT PEPPERS, BLUEBERRY PIE (1 large), CHERRY PIE (1 regular), STRAWBERRY PIE (1 regular), CHOCOLATE PIE (4 regular), RASPBERRY PIE (1 large), RICE KRISPIE CAKES (50 pieces), PEANUT BUTTER CHEESECAKE (1 large), PEPPERMINT CHEESECAKE (1 large), FRUITED JELL-O-- STRAWBERRY FLAVOR (2 large), CHOCOLATE CAKE (4 regular), PUMPKIN CAKE (4 six inch), MAPLE CAKE (2 six inch), WHITE CAKE (1 six inch), CRANBERRY PIE (4 six inch), BBQ POTATO CHIPS (5 bags), SOUR CREAM POTATO CHIPS (5 bags), PARTY MIX (10 bags), ONION DIPS (2 containers), HOT SPICY DIPS (1 large container), BEAN DIP (1 regular container), ASSORTED SODAS (50 sodas)

Now, how does that sound to you John?

Let me tell you John, I am stuffed for sure. For the past few days I am taking it easy. Light meals. Mostly I will eat a good breakfast and skip the rest of the day. Well now, my radio decided to play again! I had it under the bed for a while. COUNT TIME AT 4:41PM. About time for supper too. I am listening to the news as I am typing. A female sergeant just came in wiggling her ass as she walks. A LESBIAN! She has 22 years in the system and has three to go before retiring and living out her pussy licked mouth. hahahaha She is pissed off at the old man, the one that is leaving. He got her into trouble for not making her rounds in the Law Library after 6PM. Now she is there first thing after 6pm but not when the inmates are there. She got written up again just for that reason. She tried to get several inmates to say this man was asking questions on security. When it got back to the man he in turn asked that the Sergeant produce her witnesses. She refused. Security wrote her up. One more and she is gone from here! But I informed this man to sit with me at 9PM and wait for this woman to show up on her rounds of this unit at that time.

I am eating my supper of rice with mixed vegetables and steamed hamburger meat. Looks like PUPPY CHOW! It's what I get on a diet. I dumped it as I am not hungry. I'll make a cup of hot cocoa instead.

Did you hear about the Cajun country's MOST WANTED RODENT? It is the Nutria. It has overrun Louisiana's coastline and is eating all the vegetation and the soil is going into the Gulf! So there is a bounty of $4.00 per tail. Wish I was out there and caught a bunch of them. They are good eating as well and taste like rabbit. Haha MARSH RABBIT that is. They range in weight between 10 to 22 lbs. That is a LOT of rodent! ONE BIG RAT!!! Another thing I didn't know of is the Daddy long Legs does not spin a web. They are NOT a spider! They sure look like one to me! Haha A BROWN RECLUSE looks like a Daddy Long Legs except that they have two sections to their body and the Long Legs do not.

How much snow have you gotten over your way? Tell me John, have you heard from Maria? I have not in quite a while! They come and they go without ever saying goodbye!

There is trouble brewing in this unit between the smaller guys and some bullies! It keeps on and one of the bullies is going to get stabbed or have his throat cut!

I have three women to write overseas. One in Austria, England, and Norway. Which one should I indulge first John? They are all Plain Janes but better and better. Right now I have ten active women writing to me. I lost quite a few of them for one reason or another. But new ones are always popping up.

The temperature is going down into the teens tonight. With a serious wind chill factor. Bad to be out tonight without proper clothing for sure. Get with someone and keep warm...

My book of choice this evening is WINTER MOON BY DEAN KOONTZ. I've read most of his books but missed this one.

Time to shut down and turn down the lights. Be good John or be good at it.

TAKE IT EASY BUT IF IT IS THAT EASY TAKE IT TWICE! hahaha

LATER PAL

ART

"Mr. Fay, you now have her photos. Do as you wish with them."

A curious thing to write, certainly, and I did have a fair enough idea of what my new friend Shawcross was suggesting. It was the strangest of feeling-out process between the two of us. The man was hinting that I should... maybe find and make this woman, apparently having annoyed or offended him, disappear. At least, it wasn't an order, only a vague suggestion. Like a "Dear Santa/Satan" wish list of sorts. Of course, it wouldn't have mattered either way. Even if I were inclined to track this woman down, I didn't have the funding to begin going on murder trips around our otherwise lovely United States. The matter was never pressed, I was grateful, but it was something permanently branded into the background, officially putting our relationship at the far end of the deadly serious spectrum for hardcore hyper-drive, four-point-restraint dangerously weird. Part of me couldn't help but to fall in love with the guy for the subtle wickedness in his suggestions.

Though, I took it all in stride and decided to go with the flow (and don't ask what was flowing--every answer is a bad one). What else could I do? Having invited demons into my life when I was ten years old, this was what I ended up with. You get what you pay for.

As a dubiously funny note about selling or compromising one's soul is how addictive it can be, once you realize how effective and pragmatic a solution it really is. Then, pretty soon, you find yourself offering whatever is left of your soul just to find your house keys (which, incidentally, is the fasted way to find them if you happen to be in a hurry, even if you will burn in Hell for it later).

It's so raw and absolute in its purity of power, flooding the mind and spirit. It's irresistible. A unity with something so beyond yourself, something so sacred and untouched. Something not human at all. Spreading out past all horizons and preconceived ideas of limits, and comforting in its tranquilizing assurance that it has everything under control. And, above and beyond everything else relating to human consumption and collection, isn't that the principal point: control?

Concepts of order. To bring calm out of the confusion and make the subject safe--whereby the one highlighted in the chaos of the crowd can't ever be tainted again--by way of an inversion of birthing. The death knell closes doors for most but bursts doors open for others. The ones whose imagination has somehow deviated and become Deep Web material. The truly scary ones. Often, it presents as a whirling blackness that shuts everything else out. You can be walking in a hustling city of the autopilot people and hear nothing but the isolating wind of the gruesome desert in the eye of an ominous tempest, whispering its poetic recommendations for seizing controlling interests in an apocalyptic dynasty of horrors.

It's a systematic divesting of humanity and emotional dissection by some methodically mad cosmic surgeon, leaving one, at best, with a very selective empathy and the rage of a ravenous mountain lion as your constant, clawing baseline. Through reptilian reasoning, sympathy and empathy are recognized as potential death sentences for the self. One may seek that mythical help, perhaps, but never say more than you talk yourself out of.

Since the age of fifteen and into my mid-twenties, like reels of film running by an internal wall of eyes, frozen in a permanent trance, intrusive but inexplicably welcome images of getting and keeping (mainly, keeping) the archetypes of the Goddess, the Cheerleader, the Princess (maybe even a good-looking nun added to the ingredient list to satisfy any Equal Rights hang-ups). It's a twisting of the human affinity for collecting things. An oddly sentimental mind.

The Naval psychologist who mercifully deemed me unfit for the service was understandably treating me with kid gloves when I was in his presence. ("Are we feeling better now, Mr. Fay?"). With fresh bites temporarily disfiguring both arms, I sat by myself in his outer office lit gently with green lighting, uncertain of what the consequences of all of this would be, picturing a six-month lockdown in a military mental hospital. In the discharge papers, according to how I described it to the psychologist and my understandably dumbfounded drill instructors on Parris Island (summer of 1997), I had, for a long time, been quietly entertaining "Jeffrey Dahmer type fantasies." Playing with occult magic as a boy, I might've inadvertently installed some kind of demon malware into my thinking; I never knew for certain where such thoughts came from. But they were there, all the time. My arms always seemed to get the brunt of things. I would later permanently scar my left arm with an especially expensive steak knife, having had occasional fits of self-mutilation when frustrated and drunk.

At the very least, I'm already predisposed to aberrant leanings and other addictive behaviors. The man who always stood out for me was an uncle, "Uncle Georgie," as the family knew him. A notorious alcoholic and legendary neighborhood eccentric, he killed several Nazis in WWII and allowed himself certain liberties as people sometimes do in such situations. He removed the gold fillings, teeth, and jewelry, of the Nazis. Later, back home, he pawned the gold to raise cash for liquor.

It has occurred to me that I hadn't been doing anything so different from George, insofar as ghoulish behaviors went. Although among family having been close with him, I was infinitely worse than him. If only I could have found some Nazis to enact my fantasies on.

There is such a great SCREAMING chasm between society and myself as the average person perceives it. As if I'm some thoroughly defiled and defiling architect of the ghastliest of ghettos obscured by permanent shadow. It toxically configures and disfigures an existence of never-ending, pervasively torturous anxiety, wickedly bizarre thinking, and fear of doing irreversibly evil things.

Hopeless, sad, desperate, destitute, and deranged at the height of my abandonment of hope, whom else could I have possibly found to take me in as a friend at the time? Who else would understand and wouldn't judge but Arthur Shawcross?

A writer lives much of his life in self-imposed isolation

as it is, but add to that the High Strangeness of murderous inclinations alongside a penchant for reducing human heads to roughly the dimensions of a grapefruit and problems do arise. Extreme agoraphobia and leanings toward a ghastly view of humanity have made the interactions I've experienced with people, shall I say, a uniquely tense experience. A good example of this is when I psychologically tormented and briefly stalked a delivery man with an unfortunate face whom I deemed annoying and suspiciously disrespectful which, in clearer retrospect, was probably my inflexible tendency to overthink everything. So, if you happen to be that delivery man reading this, sorry…my bad.

Surpassing that, past the gushing anxiety sweats, constant panic, near-heart-attacks, and persisting sense that people might be reading my very mind; certain thoughts are somehow too big to stay hidden after all. There is also the knowing that it represents a kind of transcendence through descent. Presenting as a euphoric sense of purifying transmutation, it's as though I'm not one of them anymore, if I ever was. Or maybe, it's just waking up to who and what I was all along, for better or curse. It's not as much a departure from humanity as a realization of never having been a part of it from the start.

Although it doesn't escape me that demons are notoriously deceptive tricksters, I would not ever underestimate their mischievous inkling to provoke damnable acts or to provide me with a zip-line right down into damnation. It's almost like having siblings incessantly instigating problems and bringing the whole house down on your head. Only, from a supernatural or preternaturally perverse vantage point. Bargaining with the Devil, in my opinion, is a reasonable alternative for those with a relaxed policy on rules and whom have become exasperated with dealing with any mainstream vision of a deity consistently late for lunch.

Just be sure to soberly scrutinize the fine-ass print, ladies and gentlemen. Every permutation of demon has eventually stabbed me in the back. The lesson learned: it pays to have a healthy paranoia. As a side note, also, never allow a drunken barber to cut your hair, nor a junkie dentist to pull your teeth.

Now that Shawcross and I were quickly finding common ground, I was beginning to be more comfortable being me and, albeit in a Crypt-Keeper-on-Meth kind of way, I felt as if I wasn't as much of an outcast anymore. Then again, if only people knew. We are, indeed, here.

Just after my twenty-fourth birthday in August of 2000, the summer of Shawcross and "honeymoon" period of our brotherhood, wrapped up with a letter expressing his own growing ease with me.

Along with my previous piece of correspondence, I'd enclosed a postcard depicting a large, broadly-grinning deer behind the wheel of car with its top down and a rifle propped up in the passenger seat. That carefree deer was dressed in a checkered hunter's outfit, hunting cap, and wearing yellow-tinted sunglasses; a dead man in similar hunter regalia was tied securely to the hood. A humorous reversal of fortunes if you will. I also attempted to send some music and spoken word audio tapes featuring William Burroughs and Charles Bukowski, but these weren't permitted at Sullivan, and classified as "contraband."

On what might be a grimmer note, I randomly broached the topic of "collecting" the homeless and the simply aimless. Certainly, nothing personal or prejudiced against such types, as I, too, became somewhat of a hobo eventually. What I discussed with Shawcross seemed appropriate at the time, and wasn't exactly "off-topic," considering the company I was keeping. What more can be said here? It is what it is. Like attracts like. Shawcross and I did talk about other things.

As of late, I had begun deteriorating into a devastating psychotic alcoholic with medical and psychiatric classifications of "SEVERE." I routinely had a daily blood alcohol content (BAC) of at least four times the legal limit, if that's any comfort. Never have I admitted this until now. Arthur Shawcross had begun to affect me in potentially ruinous and subversive ways. Even though I'd assured various people that he hadn't, he was soon in my bloodstream like a shot of slow death.

At least I still had the far-off twinkling of a functional conscience, though I remained desperate to tweak and modify it so it wouldn't be such a nag. As it is, I pace for miles and miles a day, criticizing myself for everything and anything. I was coping with the stressors of deviant concepts of reality and having to war with the vacant landscape of my morality in general. Compounding that, the implications of Shawcross sharing his often-deadly revelations with me caused a certain amount of inner turmoil. Also, and this too was important, maintaining any friendship was a nearly debilitating emotional pressure cooker and such things have always been a drain on my resources. But there is an added element of stress when you know approximately how irrational and atrociously illogical maniacs can, and eventually will, be. I should know. Antisocial personality disorder feels like a security blanket for me. That's how antisocial I am. So, it's reasonable to say that I get it. Though I do sometimes dread dealing with other crazy people, I looked forward to this one.

7/19/00

Hello John,

You can call me ART if you want. Thank you for the money order.

The stationery you chose is quite good. Reminds me of someone I knew one time. TIED UP, BLINDFOLDED, AND GAGGED is GOOD; her legs would not be tied--WIDE OPEN, I would think. My face would be right there EATING LUNCH!!!

I like blondes, brunettes, redheads, or whatever. BUT I am choosy in the type I crave. I like any female with a full-lipped pussy. A good handful. Something you can really cup in your hand. There is something about pussy lips that turn me into a SEX MACHINE! But at times I lose control and it's as if I made a SNUFF FILM. Now those would be real nice to get into!

SUITCASE PEOPLE, as you state, from an out of the way butcher shop...hanging out on roadsides, yes, folded neatly into "mild-mannered" suitcases, briefcases, duffel bags...

You forgot to mention a saw or two. MY specialty is the KEYHOLE SAW! It's what I used on THREE VICTIMS. Then you have the JIGSAW: Real handy, that!

How many days were you connected with the Service (Marines)? Ah, you bit up your arms, eh? Good thing you aren't double-jointed. HAHA

John, if you plan to sell a drawing, do so on the Q.T. If you want, we can split the profits!

Goofy, where did you get the Goofy drawing? Who bought it, do you know? I did a Goofy for one person and he said he had it on his den wall. This I'll look into!

Where there is a will you can find a way! If by chance you see something of mine being sold, please let me know who's who?!

I sent in an appeal this morning again for my supplies. I spoke to the Deputy of Administration. And he said he didn't get my letter. YA RIGHT!

A severed head does have a certain CHARM to it. At least you could get head without being BITTEN! HAHA

Why did Ebay close you down? OK, BOOTLEG VIDEOS. On what subject were they? Try "SAWWW MAN.:"

O.J. didn't kill Nicole--his FRIEND did!!! Think about it--he ALSO had a white Bronco....It's very strange it was gotten rid of right away. So you tell ME?! Something worth looking into!

Taxes are destroying this country.

What is wrong with you, John, sick? Bipolar Disorder. Manic and Depressive. A NERVOUS WRECK. If you want to live in desert country, make sure you have water. Try for either solar energy or even wind. Self-sufficient. Pick up a girl, take her home...Look for a CAVE.

If the U.S.A. ever thought of going to war with China, they would LOSE! How many Chinese are in this country today? MILLIONS! You can't fight a war within your own borders and elsewhere at the same time...

There is a new bomb being made that is better than NUKES. It kills but leaves the area clean--NO RADIATION! NO HARMFUL AFTEREFFECTS.

John, at the top of the ear is a nerve that goes around the back of the head to the other ear. This area swells up to the size of your thumb when I have a headache! That, my friend, is PAIN--even my EYES hurt then!

Caught between the platform and tracks: yes, I have heard of this. But I've never been on a train of that sort. Only out in open areas. Hop in, hop off, hobo style. One never stands too close to the tracks when the train comes in! But people do just THAT. WHAT IS THE RUSH? John, I've seen a man get stuck in a coupling of two cars. He died when the cars were pulled apart. But while in there he felt no pain! His family were sent for. A real SHOCKING SIGHT...

This week I'll try more ink art. At the moment, my left hand is sore.

I miss going to rummage sales. You meet interesting people. If you know what to look for you can make money at it. Gold, silver, sterling silver, old items.

Give me a big U.F.O. and fill it with women to do what I tell them or out the door they go. Make sure you have robot guards. HAHA! Robots obey without question!

I just ate a tomato with lots of black pepper on it. Pepper we are not allowed. Got a catalog with pork products. What tastes better than pork?

PUSSY...

Gotta Go Pal,

* * *

8-13-00

Hello John,

I hope all is well with you as well can be.

Now, MR. SAWMAN, how well did you do on the eBay selling my Birds sketch?

I have the earphones, thanks. In this letter is the receipt signed with your name on it as the one who bought the earphones.

I'll have my art supplies returned to me this week. Could have had them days ago but one sergeant is out sick.

What I may do is donate several drawings to the art show at Albany, New York. Only you and one other have the Birds drawings.

A letter came in last evening from Sweden. A very sexy woman. REDHEAD at that--and with a SHAVED PUSSY. She has been here in 1998. Man, I was IN there--FINGER LICKIN' GOOD. This one has a heck of a tongue action when kissed, too! Such is life is right. Makes a man ROCK HARD! HAHA

Lots of work to do when I get going. I have to order pencils, erasers, sketch pads, canvas, canvas panels, brushes, paints, pens, glue, tracing pads, vinyls, masking tape, Scotch tape, oils--oils are what cost so much. Acrylics are good but dull in color. Plus other items. Some things I can no longer buy--so I'll MAKE them or get them on the "UNDERGROUND SYSTEM" Black Market. We can longer buy Q-Tips, so I'll make them. Q-Tips are good for shading. The bad part is that we are allowed only 16--two ounce bottles of paint or in tubes. But this can be daily if it is done right.

Get back to me when you're able.

Later,

Art

By now, Shawcross and I were rapidly establishing a reasonably friendly camaraderie and overall understanding of each other like some secret and severe sideshow. Of course, one parcel of common ground is our mutual interest in human heads. You can't advertise for friends like this, you just kind of find each other.

Shawcross and I agreed that there was a certain enchantment which a head---shrunken, mummified, desiccated, shaken, or stirred--tended to carry with it. Heads had their own special aura. My thus far murderless obsession probably took it a step or so further conceptually, which, no doubt, added to the substance of our exchanges. It wasn't like I had anyone else with whom I could discuss such deliciously tasteless things.

To return to my experiences while on Parris Island, South Carolina, Marine Corps boot camp in the summer of 1997, and how it came to a forty-car pileup of an abrupt end. After dealing, rather poorly I admit, with many perceived stressors just about three months into basic training, I engaged in a bit and bite of auto-cannibalism. Heartily, I chomped and chewed on my forearms, drawing substantial streams of blood until I elicited the attention of my drill instructors. The senior DI, shaking his head in disgust, disbelief, and exasperation promptly sent me over to the office of the Naval psychologist. In the end, I was given an "Uncharacterized Discharge" and then put on a bus back to Boston. They gave me a bus ticket and six hundred dollars accrued since I'd gotten there. Auntie Lorraine had mailed down a credit card that she acquired with my name just in time while I was in the casualty unit waiting for the necessary paperwork to go through on the discharge. I was blessed to be able to detour once they let me out and catch a flight, sparing me what would've most definitely been an intolerably grueling twenty-four-hour bus ride.

The training, at least, hadn't been unreasonable. I had trained in martial arts throughout my life but I couldn't swim.

So, when the time came to qualify in the boot camp pool for survival swimming, I was an above average drowner but that didn't impress the instructors. It would be my downfall for that experiment. My hopes for suicide by proxy were dashed. The prospect of being recycled several weeks was a very real one. And then still not being able to swim made it seem to me that I didn't have many choices.

It was a relief returning to Boston. Even if the elation of my re-discovered freedom would soon wear off. It usually does when coming out of any kind of incarceration or fornication. And, as usual, another odyssey of derangements wouldn't be far behind.

August 15, 2000, was the first birthday of mine Shawcross and I would (in some sense) spend together. Through simple synchronicity, he happened to write me on the dubious anniversary of my worldly introduction, born to parents who would not only wish but attempt a belated abortion numerous times. Including the very late-term abortion attempt by way of my father trying to back over me with his Cadillac one night. Shawcross was a pleasure to deal with by comparison. He wrote me two letters two days apart, and I was pleased with the degree of friendship that was quickly coming to be.

8/15/00

Hey John,

Jeffrey Dahmer was into eating, torturing, and fucking his homosexual partners. As for me, I only ate CERTAIN parts: CLITS. Quite tasty at that. Don't need salt either!

Cunt tastes good most times--some smell like tuna, sardines, soap, and perfume, and musky too! But I've had the displeasure to get close to one that was full of CRABS. A little bit of KEROSENE on that bitch got her to screaming in her gag--while tied up. Pull the panties down to ankles. Remove one leg, twist panties twice, and re-insert leg. Push legs and ankles back so you hook the panties behind the head. A trussed-up turkey--pussy wide open--asshole too! Pour on the kerosene and watch those crabs die. Shave that cunt close--smooth. The bitch was lucky I didn't set it off with a match!

My stepdaughter will not have a can of tuna in the house! "CUNT IN A CAN," she calls it. I had to ask her how does she know that cunt smells like tuna. HAHA She stated she has one and I asked, can I check it out for a tuna smell? HAHA Hell, NO, I was told. Woe is me...HAHA

John, if you want a woman to fuck for the winter, pull one of the homeless. She will like it inside all winter. Give her a dick to suck and fuck. Then in the Spring, let her go. I've been there. All winter with two women in the apartment!

If a guy asks a woman for a piece of ass, does he cut off a chunk or fuck her in the ass? Most of them will tell you that a piece of ass is pussy fucking. A trick of words.

SNUFF FILMS do exist. I have performed in several. My eyes were the camera.

Ed Gein's last victim is just about like one of MINE. But not tied up. Mine was laying back, legs open, no pussy, with a silly grin on her mug.

Never cross-grain any cuts--MAKES FOR TOUGH MEAT! A human has to be hung upside down and bled out while in a warm condition. Then skinned and chilled for 24 hours. Then cut up into choice cuts. CUT THE RIBS IN HALF. There is an art to cutting up a human. First, you make the MAJOR CUTS and then remove several things like FAT, VEINS, and BLOOD. Par boil each section first. Bake or deep fry. Simmer in sauces.

A human 16 to 28 years of age is best.

John--THE SAWWWWWW MAN--every human, no matter what color, looks the same after they're SKINNED.

When you hold open a door and get no thanks--you CLOSE IT QUICK! HAHA

The headphones sound good, THANKS. Can't wait to hear subliminal stuff. Some subliminals stop people from smoking--need one for a good ORGASM. HAHA COOL.

My art supplies were given back to me! Now I can get busy. I can do another Goofy or several of them. John--can you tell me where that one Goofy came from? I only made two Goofys and need to know who sold it. Man, if another guy pretends to be a female I'll KILL him or have him KILLED SLOWLY--DICKLESS, BALL-LESS!

John, if you go to Southern Cal, stay away from any earthquake section. STAY OUT OF LA OR SAN FRAN! "AIDS" Let's you and I waste some morons!

Be cool, pal. Don't hurt anyone. At least don't get caught at it.

Good day.

Art

* * *

8/23/00

Hello John,

Those tapes you sent me were confiscated as contraband. NO HOMEMADE TAPES. All have to be NEW! I was informed to let you know these are not allowed. More than likely they will listen to them.

Another thing, John: please, in the future, don't send website printouts. Just mention the items we spoke of.

I do not care to be associated with Gacy or Bundy.

MR. SAWWWWWMAN. We can make a song on that. HAHA

Check on a Taylor out of Hamilton, Ontario, Canada.

Has anyone heard of this person -- male or female???? Quite demanding. No driver's license. Jealous I get contact visits with other females and is pissed off I am married.

John, this may be a woman who wants to feel important if she married me and hit the talk shows. This I don't need.

Just call me "THE EATER MOSQUITER". HAHA: I bite for REAL. Suck up your blood and leave you empty of LIFE. SLURP SLURP...Cool, Man.

John, I never took one item from ten bodies but took the HEAD of one! Dorothy, Age 59. She will be forever mine...But I did eat the pussy of THREE... Anna, June, & June.

Partial to Dorothy Blackburn. Now what are the chances of getting two Dorothys and two Junes???

UNREAL! Frances swallowed the wiener -- GULP! Filisha Stevens got hooked on a car window as I DROVE AWAY...Elizabeth Gibson was HIV positive. She got nothing but PEACE OF MIND -- No medication. Patti Ives was hooked on cocaine! Darlene Trippie was a LIVING DOLL: Ball squeezer for REAL. Maria Welch was ONE HOT BROAD but was always in a hurry...But I'll see them all again FOREVER...THEY AND THEIRS BELONG TO ME ONLY...

I did not need an altar like Jeffrey Dahmer, but it sounds like I should've had one!

Kindness is a virtue. But who is to say that all people you meet are HUMAN...

I believe in ALIEN LIFE other than of this world...

You need a SPECIAL TOUCH, John. Something to touch someone and then die later in the day. COOL. There is shit on the MARKET like that!

As to cutting heads...let's go to VIETNAM. Heads come off EASY over there. No tacos! SPARE RIBS, HAMS, ROASTS, LEG OF HUMAN. Where is the Tabasco sauce and Worcestershire?

Got a letter from a Swedish gal, and a photo. Man, does she look GOOD!!!! So do the other two with her. This lady says she'll see me next years for a week. HOT

DAMN, FINGER-LICKING GOOD!

Crabs is not a disease. It's caused from being dirty and not washing properly. You can get crabs off a toilet seat. AIDS, syphilis, THE CLAP (HOLD YOUR APPLAUSE!), and other social diseases are

DEADLY... I've eaten a few crabs in MY day. HA HA

I agree on a homeless woman. Make her a deal: sucking and fucking for room and board. Bet you get one or even TWO.

California? Only Central to Northern. Stay out of southern area.

Yup, a piece of ass is cool.

Think about the theory of placing a camera on a dead person's eye. Is it possible to see what they saw last?? I created SNUFF FILMS. I had no camera, only my eyes.

THEATER OF THE MIND!

Put 'em under, revive them many times. DRAG IT ON -- USE CPR.

There is NO Heaven or HELL. But if there IS, I get to kill them over and over again, forever!

Some CUNT out of Kentucky owes me $50.00! And I'll be looking for her RIGHT PROPER -- with INTEREST! She'll get her comeuppance very SOOOOOOON...I've got a special messenger who lives not far from her ass.

She bought one of those two-seater cars. Gee, NO BRAKES, how NICE!

I am big all over. When I lift weights, the guards pay attention. I pulled a muscle in my left hip. No pain, no gain. I can pop 320 lbs. You should see that bar BEND!

The deer postcard is cool. Cute. I've seen one deer get a hunter. Fucked him up BAD!

No head, no hands, no feet! I'd cut off the arms near the shoulder, legs at the hip, leave the head for SPORT. What a fuck that would be.

Be cool my brother,

Art

CHAPTER THREE

TWisTED
One bright morning
In the middle of
The night
Two dead boys got up to
Fight.

Back to back
They faced
Each other,
Drew their knives
And shot each other.

A deaf policeman
Heard the noise
And came to arrest
The two dead boys.

If you don't
Believe
This tale is true,
Ask the blind woman,
She seen it all TOO...

Shawcross didn't actually write this poem. It seems that even when you are a world famous serial killer, at times you like to try and put on airs. It wasn't the first or the last time he attempted to pawn off others' writing as his own.

I was fifteen years old in 1991, the year Jeffrey Dahmer was taken into custody for the murders of what turned out to be seventeen young men and boys. The apprehension of Dahmer perfectly coincided with my own formative idiosyncrasies. The season of sacrilege had begun. It was a most unusual and disturbing synchronicity. Carl Jung himself would've been nauseated with astonishment, and I am a Freudian wet dream come true.

The spell that binds and weirdly mesmerizes is twilight of the heart. A hostile takeover of the soul punctuated by interspersed, explosively invasive visions of cascading blood, perverting what should've been healthy sexual moments into libidinously implosive ground zeroes.

One of the most astounding realizations of my life was that Dahmer and Shawcross actually liked people! After all, people are very delicious.

I've picked up on an imperative to digress. There's no entirely effective way to deal with slipping into such an exotic strain of derangement while also going through puberty, as I was when the affliction noticeably started to affect my thinking. Directing these weird energies becomes a full-time job (and I hate full-time jobs). But there is never such a loss of touch with reality that it suddenly makes sense to discuss these matters with anyone else not in a similar boat. It's important to further emphasize--in case there is a need to clear up any doubts as to my inborn allegiance to certain underbelly forces and the more out-to-lunch jinn kin and ambiguously-allied angels--that there's no denying I am the afflicted. The only difference with me is it didn't go the final, crucial period that labels one as such. Although, I was at the edge and, in the end, was flailing in the same abyss I'd enjoyed sailing on for most of my days, living and dying with its terrible tides.

It just occurred to me one day. Seemingly, all of a sudden, though, I'm sure, after an initially subtle progression. This force of the preternatural had probably been in the process of boiling to the point of bubbling over and scalding anyone nearby for quite some time. Curiously, however, there is an incongruous gentleness to its consumption of one's life; a soft, but toxic, kind of otherworldly lovemaking. I recognized this later in life as a ghoulish grooming process. And then, there is an awakening to a vivid, coaxing beacon of annihilation, implicitly promising a kind of inverted rapture: a purifying of weaknesses, vulnerability, and anything profane; a fast-track VIP ride right to the end of the rainbow. Here, dreams don't merely come true, they become YOU.

I knew that there was nothing and no place more godless, but it was a world which I owned, an exhilarating, labyrinthine domain of majestic shadow, tranquilizing starlight, and the electric titillation of possibility. It's a rush of an accessible power--not promised but self-evident--having plugged directly into to the source, perhaps, of everything that motivates all precipitation of death and the deepest recesses of depravity. It's the very hub of the ones who invented bloodshed itself. The place where Creation went mad.

Maybe the most troubling part of it was the whispers.

Agitation and resentment bring them to the surface, speaking more to the intuition than the intellect. The whispers aren't straight English, or any decipherable verbal language, but something hacking into a savage instinct that should never have been allowed introduction into any civilized society (or reasonable facsimile thereof). I've found myself nodding in acknowledgement of them (sometimes in public, self-consciously catching myself, hoping nobody noticed) and of their messages I intuited. As a general guideline of mine, I keep it to myself because it's much too terrifying to relate whatever they suggested. However, this is necessary for record, posterity, and the potential to help anyone battling with these horrors. The central theme of the whispers is usually along the lines of "kill them all." Suggestions, or recommendations, more than orders or anything actually insisting that I override my determination not to be shipped to some subterranean cage, where I'd find myself beating my head against a very unforgiving cell door and attempting suicide for breakfast every day of my thirteen-hundred-year-with-good-behavior bid.

Some of it is fueled by a general frustration of perceiving others as living more palatable lives than I. Especially those in what at least seem like fairly consensual relationships. Seeing people that seem to possess that man-woman dynamic which eludes me for years at a time is not only an irritant but, in fact, something that deteriorates my mood very quickly. That's not the only thing, but it doesn't help. And then, there are just the human pukes who get under my skin for something that appears irrelevant. Something like this might move me to start shopping around for a nice ax (or even a handy crucifixion kit). But these are scenarios that, if brought to life, would get anyone sent upstate and underground. Out of sight, man, and out of my mind, legally stuck where the sun never shines.

It could manifest in the oddest of ways, literally bleeding into the common reality. Once, when my parents were showing their house to a lady and gentleman couple who were house shopping, it hadn't occurred to me to take down the wall of death scenes I'd taken out of innumerous true crime publications. Not exactly "soft core" material, either: men and women cut in half, beheaded, thoroughly-grotesque dismemberments, strung upside down, shotgunned, smashed by trains, all available pictures of Dahmer's catches (photos Dahmer had snapped in Apartment 213 himself with his Polaroid, the photos later confiscated by Milwaukee Police), a collage of Ted Bundy victims, Ed Gein's permanent guests--and the offenders themselves: Dahmer on the cover of People and Newsweek framed and hanging nearby all of the atrocities I'd somehow decided made the room feel more cozy.

Honestly, I can barely begin to imagine what dread was turning over in the minds of those prospective buyers or what they could've possibly been thinking. A surprise to me, though, how stoic they kept themselves. They deserve points for maintaining their composure, I guess. The husband kept a respectful distance from the room on that otherwise lovely Saturday afternoon in autumn, 1995. It was kept dark in there, the only light filtering in through the curtains of the room's only window facing a gigantic pine tree. The wife, oddly, seemed to indulge her curiosity in this very private gallery of mine. I was already mad that they were both taller than me (that irritated me for some reason). But this was before I got into drinking, so nobody lost their legs over it or was otherwise summarily cut down to size. That should be another rule: Do not amputate the limbs of prospective buyers (of anything you might be selling).

This wasn't a situation that I was "getting off" on. Quite the opposite, it felt like a violation. It's just that I hadn't planned ahead well enough. That would be a recurring problem in my life. Admittedly, shocking people is usually an invigorating pastime but it needs to be something on my terms, in my time. While they were there, I quietly stayed in the background, hoping that nobody would ask me anything obnoxious like the ever-popular, "Do you see a therapist?" What could I have said? They could've freaked, ran out, even called the police (the cops were called with some regularity to that house anyway due to a menu of domestic disruptions). There wouldn't have been any charges, but it would've made things unnecessarily awkward. Possibly, at worst, I might've been committed to a psychiatric hospital. As it was, though, the wife--probably in her mid-thirties and used to suburban life--did seem to have taken a certain amount of polite interest in the pictures. She briefly scanned each one but never said anything about them. It was a surreal experience. I've found that women are funny that way. They didn't buy the house, either.

I started my shrunken head collection around the time when my correspondence with Shawcross began…

To be further truthful, part of my reasoning for pursuing a writing career is in the hopes of buying a new collection of heads. The online world, and especially eBay, had opened up a wonderful dimension for me. Bored and lonely, in the living room of the dollhouse one night, on a whim I typed "SHRUNKEN HEADS" into eBay's search engine. Immediately, I was mesmerized, while also recognizing how much of life I had missed out on, thus far.

The concept itself of taking a human's head and devising a way to shrink said head is, I still think, a resounding exclamation of the grim majestic. There is something so regal about the shrunken head. An elegant and ingenious summation of the macabre and the quintessential symbol for my own black magic heart. The brilliance of the workmanship and the care put into the heads is undeniable. I quickly fell acutely in love with these artistic masterpieces of the atavistic.

As far as I know, and according to all disclaimers, the heads were "ONE OF A KIND!" and "Museum Quality" replicas. Translate that as thou wilt. I think it may fall under the arcane category of ARTS & WITCHCRAFTS. Most definitely, what was offered to the highest bidder were amazingly realistic renditions crafted with exceptional attention to detail. Such as the ears. The ears are very important when it comes to shrunken heads. Because of the intricate shaping of the human ear, they are among the qualifiers to determine the authenticity of a head or the caliber of a faux head. The nostrils and nose hairs are another (look for hairs). If too good, a head may be more real than legally allowed (allegedly). The seller in Florida making the replicas that I'd won from his eBay auctions was a passionate artist who had obvious love for his work. Such fastidious attention to detail. He constructed his pieces with skins from various animals, often adding ***REAL*** **Human Hair!** (as was featured on eBay). Hair from a human being is of course far easier to procure than, say, an actual human face.

The heads the Floridian master craftsman of sideshow gaffs made were not the cheap, mass-produced, goatskin knockoffs. Each was an original and I primarily bought my heads from him. He referred to me as, "Hands down, my best customer." In case the multitude of financial institutions having loaned me money were ever concerned about my having mindlessly squandered their thousands of graciously proffered dollars, there was clearly never a need for concern. Shrunken human heads are a unique, once-in-a-lifetime investment opportunity. The cocaine is another issue.

The replicas were modeled after "tsantsa," as the South American natives referred to the severed heads from tribal enemies they absconded for esoteric and sentimental reasons. Curiously, during one period in history, shrunken heads were so fabulously popular as conversation pieces to display in the home that a cottage industry of "counterfeits" popped up. Often, these were made by unscrupulous but enterprising medical doctors using materials from unclaimed bodies in whichever morgues they had access. The nearest I knowingly got to this was a head purportedly made from a human scalp I'd won at auction after a vicious bidding war. That acquisition was the centerpiece, of those accumulated after several months, in a black-and-white Polaroid picture I snapped of the closest semblance to a loving family I'd probably ever have.

The procedure, under the usual conditions, for shrinking a head is a process involving the methodical removal of the skin, face, and scalp with hair, from the skull. Next comes the conscientious boiling and simmering of the skin down to a reduced state, while one affectionately makes sure not to boil to the hair out. Like some savage surgeon, then, diligently molding the facial features until they resemble the man or woman as they were in life. Important to keep the hair intact. An artisan's skill, although hardly marketable these days (on the open market, anyway).

Separate from eBay, but from the same Floridian seller (I kept in touch with the man for years), I acquired three or so full-sized mummified heads (replicas) that he sold to me with sophisticated wooden display stands like the ones he'd included with the tsantsa.

When my money was thinning out about as detrimentally as all the brain cells I was drowning in my alcoholic cesspool, I later listed some of these items on eBay, side-by-side with the original artwork Shawcross was regularly sending me. In the midst of auctioning the heads that I was willing to part with (however guilt-ridden about it as I was), one day, I was contacted by a man from the Department of Justice. First, through email and then we set up a time to talk on the phone. Although friendly enough, and rather like the woman having stumbled across my wall of death via the Real Estate section of the newspaper, probably dumbstruck, it seemed that the man working for the DOJ was feeling me out, doing his part in determining whether I was making the rounds cutting people's heads off for resale on eBay.

And the voice of Shawcross carried on throughout it all.

10/4/2000

Hello John,

I guess you did it again. Another confiscation. PLEASE, NO MORE, OK?! The bullshit I went through is too damn STRESSFUL! Let me explain further. Cassette tapes are wrapped like a cigarette pack in cellophane or near about.

I wrote a letter a while ago but got no reply. I'd thought you had made that move you spoke of.

I am back to painting and finished one two days ago on vinyl. Another one started for my wife. The first is a jungle scene with parrots, ducks, deer, frogs, butterflies, and lizards. Lots of orchids, coconuts, and palm trees. Also, bamboo scattered here and there. Even a waterfall and a volcano as background. That one will enter in the art show next spring.

Quite a few people are sick here. Colds--like flu. I had to use an asthma spray to breathe. I could not get my breath from coughing. Now, at the moment, I feel good again. Stronger. This hits me only late in the year. I see the doctor on the sixth for a look-see on a hernia, lower left side. When I cough or sneeze it HURTS! I can walk ok on a level, but to climb stairs is a BITCH for real.

Need some POONTANG. Where, oh where can it be?! HAHA!

How are you doing?

Several people have been transferred to other prisons. What is called "ROTATION OF THE TROUBLE MAKERS."

I am checking out the news on the radio. This evening I'll check out the library. I do so most every Wednesday evening. Haven't we had enough bullshit out of Bushes? Neither Bush nor Gore really run this country. ADVISORS DO!!!!! You agree or get SHOT ...

One of the guys in here got busted for something. Then he had to go take a urine test. Call me--I'll give up some piss. I am told I am too willing!

Yesterday I got a postcard from a gal out in Washington State. A nice sexy redhead, but MARRIED: Oh well, that never stopped an old dog like me ... HAHA

I haven't done any drawing lately. Busy painting. I

do have a sketch of Princess Diana for sale. This may go to the art show also--$500! I have to charge that much because someone would only put it on the internet and. get more for it. I did want to get some cards made. But I need to buy some vinyl sheets.

A magazine came in where I finally saw a picture a picture of Charlie Manson with no hair or beard. Better with hair. HAHA Old Charlie is looking to get married. Wonder who he chooses...

John, please, no more tapes. These fucking people are a pain for real. This is my second warning from them. But I do thank you for trying.

Later,

Art

Our relationship was not without its humorous moments. It seems I'd gotten my friend into trouble with his minders at least twice within the first few months of our linking up, and he sent me the confiscation slip from the prison to further emphasize the fact. I found Shawcross to be surprisingly forgiving with me. Incarceration of any kind never needs to be made more of an imposition, uncomfortable, or inconvenient than it already is, so any irritation with me would've been entirely justifiable. I'd made the earnest effort to send some music and spoken-word cassettes, as usual not following the protocol Shawcross had already outlined once. Of course, this was when my drinking pastime and other chemical dabblings were gaining warp-speed into a privatized career of self-destruction, so I wasn't following too many instructions anymore of any sort.

Between the substance abuse and the serial killer who was seemingly helping elucidate my own expressions of transgressions and borderline evil, there was an impending sense of absolute surrender. Were any inquiring minds to have occasion to pickaxe my brain on the subject of how I could link souls with such an imposing butcher as Shawcross, it was standard for me to downplay it. When one has thoughts such as mine, one becomes adept at a precocious age at hiding or otherwise camouflaging them. A necessary business arrangement, I told them, nothing more. Not that I'd lie, only omit. Why admit when you can omit? Over time, and not much of it, I became a grandmaster of omission. The reputation I'd unintentionally been gaining was chilling enough for anyone who knew me or knew of me through the horrors and rumors of horrors; both written, auctioned, and carried out.

At least, Shawcross hadn't left me stranded as most everyone else had done. The ones who couldn't leave installed more locks on all their doors. Like my dearest cousin Michelle, who was renting an apartment with her husband. Things were fine with her until everyone made such a fuss about my demonstrating a very simply-applied jiu-jitsu chokehold on him during one of those dreamy and disconnected evenings which were becoming so common for me.

Even my aunt, who was near as much of an enabler as Shawcross in her own peculiar and unintentionally perverted way would eventually start locking her doors because of me.

The mailman, though, however quietly perplexed, kept on hand-delivering the most prominent voice in my head. Remember: sometimes the voices are real.

CHAPTER FOUR

BROTHERHOOD OF GHOULS

Jails, institutions, and death. Certain programs list these in an attempt to discourage using drink and drugs but those were, honestly, the best parts for me. Not only does each build character (especially death) but all provide occasion for confession.

Before I submerged myself deeply into daily liquor soaks and black baptisms in red rivers, my routine constituted heading over to Dunkin' Donuts and finding a quiet place to sit with the most ridiculously large coffee they offered every time a letter from Art came in. It seemed appropriate enough, as Shawcross also used to unwind at Dunkin' Donuts in Rochester, New York. Incidentally, he would do this mid-murder spree, and even chat with the detectives working the case of the women who kept turning up dead locally. It was a thrill to read Shawcross's correspondence amidst people whom were blissfully unaware of the demon that I was carrying around with me in a business-sized envelope (and certainly, weren't aware of the ones calling my own heart "home"). Intentionally, at times, I left the envelopes with the prison address clearly marked out in the open on the table where I was sitting so other customers or workers might catch a horrified glimpse. Caffeine, too, like alcohol and other drugs, affected me differently than most. As one psychiatrist warned me, even a simple cup of coffee might "turn up the volume" on whatever was happening in my mind. And sometimes, it's just fun to fuck with people.

10-13-00

JOHN,

This old man is one sick dude.

Got a cold and it's bad. My chest feels like I am breathing through steel wool. I drink tea with tea and lemon. At night before bed I eat an onion with hot sauce to make me sweat under the covers. Feels like a flu!

I am sorry that those tapes did not get in! It's who you know in here. Some guys get most anything but he has to be at the package room alone with no one else around. Right -- all tapes must have the wrap on them like the store sells them.

On that other letter that you missed, I don't remember just what I said in it. Most likely on my B.S. in here.

My room is all packed up to move to another unit. D-SOUTH -- the R.S.A.T.: A violence program over here, if you can believe THAT one. Something I have to take so I can get a trailer visit with my wife. She is not getting any younger. Neither am I.

I had a pleasant surprise in the mail -- My daughter wrote me. I am truly missed and loved. Parts of the letter you can see that she was crying while writing it.

John, I weigh near 300 lbs. My daughter weighs 234 lbs. Like father, like daughter. My grandchildren miss me too.

*Twisted -- YOU??? *Smile*... One poem I wrote is titled "TWISTED". So, who is REALLY twisted? HAHA I've included a copy.*

I have those paintings done. Working on two more. Time consuming but where am I going??! The new rule is that half of the sale price goes to the Crime Victims Fund. So to make ends meet I up the price because I know that whoever buys them will turn around and sell them on the eBay for a high price and get it. My work is full of detail and color. Man, you should see the one I am doing now! Very nice. But putting in detail puts me in a sort of trance. Then when I look up my eyes tear.

Give me those Jap women from the pictures you sent and let me fuck them first. THEN cut their guts out. You and I will take over and BUTCHER WHAT IS LEFT. New restaurant -- called HUMIE. HAHA Sounds Japanese, right?

Blonde pussy and Red pussy I love to suck on! Chew the fat, so to say!

Shrunken heads: SHIT, shrink the whole body!

George Bush will take the U.S. to WAR in the Middle East over oil and Human Rights. The United States is not supposed to be a DICTATOR to the WORLD! No wonder the Arabs call us the GREAT SATAN! United we stand -- Divided we fall -- all will not stand at all...

Talk later Sawman,

Art

TRICK OR TREAT

10-29-00

Hi John,

I must say when you go out to get a LITTLE HEAD you go to EXTREMES. HAHA They look real to ME!

Oh, I've come across a few people who begged me to kill them. Those I left alone for the most part. Man, I did fuck with their minds, though. Put them to sleep and wait for them to wake up, tied up in a ready position. That black prostitute didn't agree with my weirder maneuver. She sort of croaked along the way. I did not know if she was going to rob me or what. But I robbed her instead better yet. Rubbed her out for real.

What is strange is that a man spends all day working and a prostitute will take it in 20 minutes! I've taken off a few of them FOR SPITE! All you do is sit someplace and watch her moves. She will stock her boot before getting into a car. Like a found bank! You find drugs, ID card, money--most anything once you find the spot.

John, you can actually walk the streets and see people who need to be snuffed. The badasses, even the lazy S.O.B. welfare bitches. T-Rex's FIRST MEAL! I can meet certain people along a street and my whole body sweats. A certain type of woman I'd like to fuck! Hand sweats I did not get. But I did get strange sensations like sharp hearing and sight, sweaty chest, and a strong desire as a predator. HUNGRY WOLF I AM...

That second head looks like some of these fur-heads in here. I'd shrink the head first then the body up to the chin. HAHA Fuck, shrink the neighbor's head too!

Smile*

By the time I get a trailer visit I'll not be able to rise to the occasion! Loretta is nice--FAT, FAT, FAT 234 LBS, but she's mine!

If a comet was coming to Earth I'd fuck everything in sight! Might even CHEW on a few as well. Cunt is like tuna fish. If it smells bad it must be good. HAHA

Thank you for the money order, John, I sure needed it.

BE GOOD OR GOOD AT IT!

Later

Art

Advice which resonated with me every day since that letter. It was generally in undertones, that Shawcross would've supported me had I more or less followed in his footsteps. Anything is possible.

Anything.

God may have forsaken some of us, but it seems that the Devil has forever been a fan and sponsor. Sometimes all one needs to do is acknowledge these forces, show them gratitude, and doors begin opening. A succession of these doorways I ended up walking through blindly, hoping that whatever I came across on the other side wasn't scarier than I was. Arthur Shawcross wasn't necessarily scarier as far as raw weirdness goes. He was, however, something I never considered myself to be, which was purebred evil. I may be one of the darkest and most colorfully deranged characters ever to walk the streets, or wherever I happen to be taking my three a.m. strolls, but I come just short of the kind of first-tier psychopath of the man I would eventually see as a much-needed substitute father figure.

My own enchantment with collector's items like the shrunken heads is not a product of a particularly overwhelming pursuit of death and destruction, usually, but a celebration of life through an ever-warping looking glass. It's a modern-day ghoul's idea of preserving the intricacies of physical beauty and an exclusive brand of companionship. A mutation of the need to connect with another person. The degrees of death are of most germane distinction and well worth addressing lest some people make blanket judgments. Those like my father, Uncle Jerry, and Shawcross produce nothing but rotted fruit and they all leave behind dead and desolate gardens serving as sad monuments to the failures of human beings that these men actually were. For certain, the first word that comes to mind when I soberly stop to think of them is DESOLATION. It's not even something they have to put effort into doing. Everything about them is death. In my own circle, I've always maintained ideals of transformation, be it in art or murder.

As for art and murder, in the "TRICK OR TREAT" letter, Shawcross touched upon shrinking an entire body. Well, I've heard that this is possible, if one has the time, patience, and attitude of perseverance, of course. There was a "gaff" I once saw in an online display of a woman's head and nude torso shrunken to approximately one-third the normal size of a lady. Again, it is impressive work, and perfect for a sideshow setup. Remember that it's the skin which is shrunken, not the skull or bones. The natives used to discard the skulls after they'd peeled off the skin, which I find to be a waste of a wonderful complement to the shrunken heads. But not everybody thinks like me.

Speaking of companion pieces, it occurs to me that maybe Shawcross himself was a companion piece of sorts to my own life. It was a brotherhood of ghouls that could've come out of the darkest of fairytales. Though, our strains of ghoulishness did differ. Shawcross was a harsh misogynist and like the Terminator in how he operated. He wasn't respectful or graceful in what he did, how he thought, or who he was. But what he lacked in decorum he made up for with a hellish kind of charisma that might only be perceptible by fellow maniacs.

11/19/2000

Hi John,

This bottom picture sure has one hairy snatch. I'd have the bush clean! HAHA. Can't prepare a good meal with a lot of hair on it. Looks like her chest got ZIPPED for real! Bet the girl has NO HEART at all. For shame. No kidney for a pee either. Oh well, just HAMS, RIBS, & THIGHS. How does one keep it fresh?

 By keeping it ALIVE: use a red magic marker and circle the legs up to the knees; then the thighs UP TO THE CROTCH. The arms up to the elbows, and up to the armpits. KEEP HER ALIVE AS LONG AS POSSIBLE. You must put her under when you cut off a piece at a time. When she wakes up she'll flip. As time goes on she will resemble a SNAIL! She will leave a trail as she moves around. HAHA But sooner or later comes the moment of TRUTH. Get another to watch the process. A HAPPY THANKSGIVING FOR REAL!!!! Join me, John? A nice corn-fed farm gal. A city gal goes to T-REX. ALL of them! After you and I check out any prospects that might need to be stimulated! HOOKER RAIDERS, HAHA: I'd not fuck one of those! A CLAP TRAP for real!

I am told I am anti-social, but I moved in groups of people. What I did not do was mingle with drunks at parties. I like to speak one-on-one or one-on-two. Fuck one as you suck the pussy of the other...Have you ever eaten fried pork rinds? Same as pussy.

BONE SAW--Cool.

COPING SAW--Best way to cope with humans…

BAND SAW

HAND SAW

CROSSCUT SAW

KEYHOLE SAW

SKILL SAW

TABLE SAW

JIG SAW

I saw--You saw--WE saw!

Sawman (SMILE)

Park Dietz, I have something for him! If I paid that man, I'd be ok, but as he was for the DA. I LOSE! Well, he'll get his like that guy Joel Norris got his! Do I have to be fond of everyone I speak to? I was FORCED to speak to him. I did not say that much at all. He asked me if I had ever hit my wife? I asked, Did you ever hit YOURS? He stated, "We are not here to talk about me." HAHA He gave me an answer without realizing it. He DOES hit his wife! I NEVER did! But I DID spank her bare ass once for getting into the wine!

Create a gal 50 feet tall. She'll use you as a tampon.

HAHA "HELP ME!"

I was very tempted yesterday to reach out and touch something I was close to. Man, the inner feelings were right there! So was SHE! With a slight smile on her face she knew she had me in a tight fix. All I could do was lean against the door and close my eyes until the moment passed. Then hit the SHOWER!

If a comet was coming to Earth, I'd grab a good-size boat and head for a high mountain and wait! Grab a dozen gals to go with me. Tied up of course! Then after we float, cut them loose. Where can they go? You go to "ground zero," John, for instant vaporization if you really want--I'll go to the woods with my harem. It might suck later, yes, but the sucking will be so cool. Smile...

The new millennium has already started. Jesus is not coming back. OTHER space people: Big Daddy, Little Spooky might show up!

What I believe in would shock most people. Our ancestors came from the stars. Man blew himself up at least once! Will do so AGAIN! We are not alone in the universe, nor in this galaxy! I wish to go home! Not on THIS planet either...

Be Cool. Wish I was in Boston now. I'd not be there long--would go more northeast.

Happy Turkey Day!

Art

"So how many bodies are there?" the arresting officer in the passenger seat turned around to ask me, handcuffed and oblivious to the extent of problems I was now facing, with the type of directness seemingly patented by cops. Obviously, he'd seen many of the unusual items in the bunker, the apartment of doom.

My obituary might justifiably be mandated to carry a warning label:

NOT FOR THE FAINT OF HEART

A moment of clarity suddenly upon me, I do return to wondering how long I'll last before the undertow takes me down permanently. That impatiently shifting thing in the corner simply wants to absorb me.

Life itself, every heartbeat of my legacy, is a signature in blood. Usually, my own. Rituals, mutually-consensual (once again, usually) blood-letting, blood drinking, blood-laced cocktails, and a past of shortcuts (literally) to stress relief--or simply, as a quick and dirty brand of psychological warfare against whoever I happened to find especially annoying--in the form of self-mutilation, have left their marks. Then there was the summer afternoon in the bunker when best friend Mike stuck a steak knife through my left hand. All I remember is the two of us drinking and watching a movie, and then a six-inch Sharper Image blade plunged straight through my hand. It wasn't the first time the place somehow ended up caked in blood. Also, allegedly, a couple of years later, I got to stab Mike back. But it's all extraordinarily alleged and, after all, charges were dismissed. I'm ok, you're ok...I've learned that no Christmas morning, even if living with Santa Claus himself Northside, comes anywhere close to matching the joy of when witnesses don't show up to court. It's the difference between walking on air as one leaves through the front door of the courthouse and being led in shackles out the back into the mobile dog cage. Something I haven't always been able to avoid.

East Boston Times-Free Press

Wednesday, February 29

POLICE BRIEFS 3-07-2012

ARREST REPORT

John Paul Fay of 210 Everett Street, East Boston was arrested and charged with assault & battery by means of a dangerous weapon (knife).

* * *

How Now John,

What's new? I am reading the new ROGUE WARRIOR by Richard Marcinko and John Weisman. Pretty good. But you have to understand the lingo of language used--But I like it. BOOKS OF BLOOD? Don't think so. I'm into SWASTIKA by Kyle Maning, BIG TROUBLE by Dave Barry, THE BLOODING by Joseph Wambaugh, and CRITICAL JUDGMENT by Michael Palmer. I am teaching a man to speed read. A real cry baby--"I CAN'T." Smack him in the head a few times and he CAN! Goes out to the weight pile, does his thing and complains later. No pain, no gain!

A rumor going around in here--No one goes home unless they have a G.E.D. Now that I AGREE with! Guys are BEGGING to get into school. HAHA I've got mine but I'm not going anywhere...

YES to giving that woman in England my address. Maria--GRRRRRRRRRR.

I've added some cards signed by me to help the cost of the typewriter. Is it enough?

Hey, why didn't that woman fuck that horse? If she can suck two inches she can shove it up her cunt too! Now that would be a real sight to see!

My stripper is a natural. Partly shaved but has a hair heart above her snatch. What a nice cunt on her--A mouthful. "SLURP!"

Pressure points--105 to 107, I believe. One does not really strike a pressure point--More so in a finger jab and twist, a pinch here or there, I know quite a few places to make anyone do as I want them to do! You can be put to sleep with very little effort. The hollow of the throat, thumb only. Release at almost the point of unconsciousness and she will cum hard! Make numb so you can't move but you know what's going on. Now THAT, John, is the WHOLE IDEA. They can watch everything but feel NOTHING!!! It's when you give them back feeling that they shut down...

Why do people think that going to Hell is a punishment?! Going to HEAVEN to worship day in and day out is not my cup of tea. Going to Hell is not punishment per se. Bet I'll fuck SOMETHING forever...

John, I have lived before and I will again and again. That is MY belief.

Time to close up. Chow time.

Later,

Art

As I was being transported to East Boston's Station 7, a few short blocks from my bunker apartment where the alleged incident took place, the officer up front posed the question with perhaps a deliberately deceptive casualness, sounding oddly impressed, his tone almost light-hearted, "So, how many bodies are there?" Pausing briefly before continuing, he then said, "We saw the arm in your apartment."

As I matter-of-factly, feeling light-headed and somewhat out-of-body, processed my position, coming down from the booze and snorted Percocet 30s from the night leading up to this surreal disaster, I experienced the sudden off-center regret of having sold off my shrunken and mummified heads. I thought it would've been further entertaining to see the reaction of the officers. Equally casual in response, I dismissively explained that the "severed human arm" on my living room floor was a horror movie prop. That defused that and nothing more was said about too many dark possibilities to count. Although, my friend's throat and the latest pooling of blood on my floor was quite a bit more of a convoluted set of legal meanderings.

Before now, I'd routinely been able to talk my way out of damn near anything. "Irish charm," my uncle used to call it. And, as if it could keep my luck charged up, since 2000, I'd been carrying around in my wallet one of the four-leaf-clover wheels Shawcross had made for me with his and my name scrawled on its front. But, in the end, luck only takes you so far. It just doesn't pan out anymore when everyone involved looks like they've been working in a blood bank that just exploded.

One evening in 2004, I was in full-blown madman mode and went on a coke run in my uncle's Dodge Ram, for which he'd been demanding the keys back for months, to a town about thirty miles from Boston. In my frothing, alcoholic, cocaine-fiending haste, I nearly drove another car off the road. A mere nudge, as I recall. Of course, a short time later the flashing blue lights were engulfing the truck. There was that moment when I seriously wondered if it had anything to do with me. Attempted murder? Of course not! Then, as I pulled the Dodge to the roadside, I remembered that I was carrying a loaded flare gun in my coat pocket. This was to be made use of, in theory, on the not-so-off chance the deal went bad with the talking manure piles with whom I'd involved myself through another "best friend."

Not that the flare gun itself was illegal--but the circumstances had CONCEALED WEAPON chiseled all over it. Plus, naturally, I'd had a drink of morbidly obtuse proportions to calm my nerves before going out on my drug-

lust misadventure. My own private inventory of possibilities: driving under the influence, attempted homicide, and concealed weapon (on the way to see my scumbag drug dealer who was punishing me with bags of garbage and hours of run-arounds all because my sister wouldn't date him). Not that I would have voluntarily shared that information with the police. The best cocaine I ever got from him was the night he met my sister. After that, she went her own way and it was all downhill. Wishful thinking was the only reason I kept going to him until the night I got a bag of grated cheese from the prick. This very same night, in fact. I didn't have a lot of room on my plate for cops or their kidnapping operation.

When the first policeman walked up to the driver's side, I was careful to keep my hands on the wheel so he could see them (although I forgot to turn the engine off, which the cop immediately instructed me to do). He then explained why he was stopping me--not that I asked. I didn't want to know. Which rules of the road had I not violated that night? That's what I was curious about. Someone had reported that I tried to run his car off the highway, which was, of course, an outrageous accusation to make. Obviously gauging my demeanor as I explained my side, I calmly explained that I was a chronically nervous person and simply a bad driver, all of which was true. The fellow driver's purported near-death experience was, at worst, an accident, if it happened at all, which I'm sure was an overreaction.

"But you've had your driver's license for almost ten years now, Mr. Fay," the officer said in a surprisingly reasonable tone (considering he was questioning an alleged attempted road-rage murderer). At the same time, he was doing a visual of the truck's interior, shining to and fro what looked to me under stress like a caricature flashlight as big as an industrial fire extinguisher. Thankfully, it was as clean as clean could be and he seemed satisfied enough.

"That's true," I quickly agreed, forcing myself to act as easygoing as possible, similar to how one would deal with a pit bull growling under its breath with a faint, gleaming strand of drool hanging from the corner of its mouth full of ready-to-tear teeth: Stay calm, stay very, very caaaaalm, John… "But I haven't driven a lot since I got the license. I don't really like to drive. Just going to visit a friend."

"Where does your friend live?"

Under the same rock your mother crawled out from! I suddenly heard both Shawcross and me replying in my mind.

Keeping what would've been an unbelievably inappropriate cackle tucked behind my lips, I answered, "Hull, sir."

Despite his apparent satisfaction with my responses, he had me get out. Fully anticipating a stumble, at least out of sheer nervousness, I was attentive to every detail of the truck and terrain as I stepped out onto the road. Certainly, I didn't want to give them cause to think that I was any drunker than usual. Now, fortunately, the two officers didn't pat search me or seem interested in doing so. Next, standing behind the Dodge Ram and in front of the police cruisers, one of the officers reservedly asked me to recite the alphabet. I knew this was not the time to exercise my right to remain silent, lest I blow my one final chance to prove my being a responsible, sober, non-homicidal citizen. With coherence that genuinely surprised the shit out of me, I did it. "A" all the way to "Z" like the man with the golden voice. They glanced at each other and smiled, weirdly amused, and the first officer I'd spoken with had me return to the truck. One of them politely clued me in that the left rear tire of the vehicle was a bit low and I should get air into it as soon as I could. Without a doubt, another of my many close calls with the law.

Eventually, two years later in 2006, I was once again driving the Dodge when I ran into some problems. The 1988 Ram was by now scarred, marred, scratched, and dented from years of my drunken miscalculations. Uncle Jerry had maintained the vehicle--all of his vehicles--in almost perfect condition ever since he'd bought it brand new and then I got into its driver's seat. Still I hadn't handed the keys over to ever-nagging Uncle. Surfing a wave of wicked abandon, experiencing lucid visions of the world furiously burning and rolling hills made of heads severed in the traditional manner of the Samurai with Shawcross on my shoulder, I maniacally barreled through the narrow streets of East Boston.

Earlier in the day, I'd had a minor disagreement with my psychiatrist and left her for good. She explained to me that she had her boundaries. I had mine too. When I'd gone in to see her in the morning, having been chasing oxycodones with vodka all night right up to our appointment, I was stoned, mean, and reckless. And so, over what I felt was her odd refusal to let me use a lint roller on her desk, the spirit of what I told her was to stuff the prescription she'd been writing for me somewhere that would've otherwise been interesting for me (I've asked out most of my female mental health workers throughout the years, though I have never exactly been taken up on it).

In addition to that, I was irritated about not being able to get any more painkillers and so, later that night, around and around the same block I sped in the beaten-up silver Dodge. At the top of my lungs, I was practically speaking in tongues, blasting some of the deadliest music available and smashing a fist into the truck's roof. Finally losing control of the Ram, skidding on what was in the official police report as "black ice," I crashed with the dramatic devastation of the Roswell flying saucer through the garage door of an electronics business at Jeffries Point, a few houses from where I was living. No injuries to anyone, except for a small gash on the top of my head, but the truck was crushed. The first officer at the scene calmly told me, "You should be going to jail for drunk driving, you know." However, he didn't seem especially motivated to detain me and didn't press it. No arrest was made that night.

I take my blessings where I can find them. As of this writing, 2006 was the last time I've driven of my own accord because, believe it or not, I badly scared myself. Easily, I could've run somebody over, and that's a serious hit for everyone. I mean, sometimes I do think about killing people, but not in such a pedestrian manner as that. A postscript to the crash is when I was miraculously walking off, dazed but not dead or in police custody, going back to the bunker and to face Uncle Jerry sooner than later, I remembered that ... GOODDAMNIT ... my keys to everything were still in the ignition! Not only that, which was bad, but there was the almost-half gallon of rum in the back. What choice could I have had? In a panic, I turned back as the tow company had the demolished Dodge up on their flatbed. Rapid-fire explaining my plight to the tow truck driver--who'd seemed initially surly but then, to my relief, he softened--certainly, I reassured him, I would be fine climbing up onto the flatbed. Never mind that I can barely walk, see, or speak straight, sir. "These are not the droids you're looking for..." I made it, though, reaching into the wrecked cab of the Dodge to snatch the keys. And then, headed to the back, where my medicinal rum was. Especially mindful that the cops still hanging around didn't take notice, I crawled into the back. When I got to the rum, which was thankfully safe and sound, with unabashed gratitude I gave the bottle a kiss before wrapping it in a red satin blanket which had been a recurring comfort in my life for decades and that now, was facilitating a drunken maniac's haphazard, half-assed rum-smuggling subterfuge.

As for the curious incident on February 29, 2012, beneficially for me, my best friend since the seventh grade survived whatever happened--or at least, he was alive the last time I saw him. Accidents allegedly happen.

The blow of my situation had been lessened by my not having a string of police and citizen assaults and batteries on record like my so-called "victim" had. All judges involved with the case didn't seem especially eager to lock me up. Even several fellow inmates with some knowledge of the case's details said that I was the "good guy." Truthfully, for the month-long period when he was staying with me, he'd return on some days recounting how he'd just hurt someone he believed was holding dope, money, or whatever. Plus, he did, anyway, stab and impale me first. But again, who knows for sure? I've had so many blackouts...

In 2001, I met a college girl named Ava online. Whenever I had what I thought of as my monthly conjugal visit from Ava, it became one of my weirdest scrambles to make sure that the tsantsa, mummified displays, full-size human skeleton, death photos, and even the body bag I'd made into my shower curtain (an "interesting trade" with an eBay customer who worked in a morgue) were all tucked away wherever I could find space. I had to do this every month for the two years that I was quietly associating with her in the bunker. It was for the best when she graduated and moved away.

I've sacrificed most of my social life for the pursuit of a writing career and then, giving up on everything for over a decade, my alcoholic, drug-fueled menace and, somewhat more often, solace. So, eight years passed since Ava before Alyssa entered my smoldering mess. Alyssa was introduced to me when I visited a family member in one of the more civilized psychiatric facilities, McClean Hospital. She took a liking to me and it was on from there, another lopsided sleigh ride through uncertainty and despair.

By the time she appeared--my blonde, blue-eyed former high school cheerleader who'd gone a bit off the rails-- I'd auctioned or sold, sadly, the better portion of the head displays in exchange for cocaine, booze, and anything that would even remotely affect my opiate receptors in favorable ways or get me away from the rambunctious things spastically beating on the walls of my skull and the careful, calculating eyes in the corner of any room I huddled up in until I was obliged to figure out how to live again. Selling my heads didn't matter, though. I'd become the display myself. There was no masking it anymore. Corrosive substance misuse and just cartoonishly over-the-top abuse and, in my delusions, having a real-deal devil on my shoulder in the incarnation of a serial destroyer, Arthur Shawcross, I was the grimmest inversion of humanity on the block. It was a true priesthood of the Apocalypse, as the Four Horsemen lost their minds and stuck the heads of their own horses under my covers. Nothing was pretty, but ugly things were soothing for me by then.

At four months, Alyssa was the longest and most serious "romantic" relationship I'd had (a blackout romance if there ever was one). An actual girlfriend, which in itself is curious testimony to the upside of poor judgment working in my favor. But, since I was blacked out ninety-nine-plus percent of the time, I only recalled about four days of the whole thing in the end, but what a lovely four days they were. At least, doing uncanny triple pirouettes in the black ether of a never-ending night, I thought so.

The last message Alyssa sent that wasn't delivered by the police was a text. I was confusedly going nowhere trying to piece together what had driven her away, sitting in the, as always, dimly-lit bunker, just me and my madness, drowning myself in liquor, when the final few sentences she ever wrote to me summed it up: You're very scary and SICK.

Her police statement filled in whatever blanks remained. If I wasn't entirely sure what she was trying to say, zombie drunk that I was, the restraining order, delivered by a pair of policemen (one trying to keep things cool by comparing it to being like a delivery from UPS as I was signing the order on my table—woken up by my uncle escorting the two of them into my place), punctuated it rather effectively. Although, as always, it's not without its broad brushstrokes of humor.

Per the affidavit:

On or about April 1-3, 2011, John Fay tried to kill me twice. He was angered by the fact that I ordered the wrong type of Chinese takeout and I wasn't taking him seriously when he was telling me the government tried to kill him by poisoning him with chemtrails from airplanes in his backyard. He held a knife to my throat and told me he knows how to cut my head off and kill me but I am not an "anonymous" person and people know where I am and he can't go to prison for the rest of his life. In that same weekend, he put his hands on my neck and told me he knows how to kill me by snapping my neck but decided against it for the above reasons. I had to sneak out of the house when he was passed out drunk the next morning. I never wanted to see him again.

He has extreme anger management problems and is constantly throwing things, banging things, etc. He is a drug and alcohol user and is never sober. He even corresponded with a serial killer, Arthur Shawcross (who recently died) in New York, who told him he has to kill. He wants to try it out by cutting off prostitutes' heads because he thinks he can get away with it because they are "anonymous people." I am terrified of him and what he will do. He is a very dangerous man.

"(…) Arthur Shawcross (…) told him he has to kill."
--Alyssa

In the interest of richer elucidation, and a vaguely hopeful attempt at self-preservation, Shawcross did not direct me to kill.

Not exactly.

He alluded to it, however, like a motherfucker.

I can't deny that it was at least a persisting undertone in our relationship. Shawcross, for example, once mailed over photographs of a woman he'd hinted at my doing him a "favor" in relation to, which puts any friendship in a precariously gray area. But it wasn't a requirement, nor was I moved by any unfortunate sense of obligation. Already I had a full plate on my table and a sink-full of dirty dishes to wash. Dealing with Shawcross was supposed to be taking my mind off those things, not shoveling more dirt into my grave. He was such a permissive father figure, though, that, in a way, he spoiled me. It can't be emphasized enough that he accepted me for whatever I was and I did sometimes wonder what the dynamic would've been had we lived together as father and son. Shawcross was the one and only quasi-human I didn't feel like I was being blindly judged by, nitpicked, and nut-kicked. Of course, neither of us were the most "Christian" of men. True, I attended church--it was the Church of Satan, but it was a church.

Though, I created my own place of quiet contemplation. I used to watch movies, all kinds of movies, with the shrunken heads arranged in no specific order around me. I'd drink cocktails as though draining a swamp looking for a lost treasure and then projectile vomit across the apartment like the possessed incarnation of cataclysm that I was. Although I was always obsessively careful, no matter how upside down, not to let any Exorcist-homage precipitation get onto the heads. This was my sacrament. Later, I would start adding heroin to the mix. I took to heroin like clouds to the sky. It was the holiest of unholies for me.

Though I've recovered, at least for the time being, one of the most cherished memories I have (in the way that most people adore the birth of a child) is the first day I tried heroin. For the three years previous, I'd been finagling three-hundred-forty ten-milligram hydrocodones every month from Internet sources, until the DEA came onto the online scene. I took all the pills myself (no sharing or selling), and washed them down with forty-day deluges of Black or White Russians, if I even had the patience to mix the drinks. But, more importantly, it was also the first time I got to view--and actually HOLD in my very hands--an authentic, historic tsantsa head. It was presumably severed and shrunken by a proud Jivaroan warrior and dedicated head-shrinker. When I was thirty-one years old (having had a somewhat later start than the typical dope fiend), I was going to a tattoo parlor owned and operated by the man who I'd sold most of my own one-of-a-kind shrunken heads to--including the prized head carefully crafted with a real human scalp. I wanted to pay my heads a visit now.

My best friend, who later became my blood brother in a ritual of drinking each other's blood mixed with liquor, was the same running partner who it was later alleged I'd used a knife on, funnily enough. But maybe my humor blurs too many lines. Mike was my partner-in-crime-for-some-time. We'd made an unstoppable shoplifting duo during our adolescent years, and besides that, were professional drug seekers, locators, and takers. He now was seeking employment for his skills as a tattoo artist. A star-alignment of motivations, I thought, with rare elation. Inside the parlor was a museum of oddities and curiosities with unusual items from all over the Earth. Seeing what I still considered my heads in one of the glass display cases was like a visitation with my children. I couldn't help but feel a deep sorrow. Christ, I really did miss them as men pine for lost women and dead dogs, and I continue to mourn the loss of my beloved heads. But there is often hope. I've considered starting a crowd-funding campaign to raise money for at least one authentic shrunken head, if not a return of my collection or one like it. Voicing my depression in an only marginally joking tone, the shop owner went and unlocked one of the cases.

"You'll love this," he reassured me. The huge, intricately-inked man, reaching thoughtfully into the case gingerly, even lovingly, took hold of what I suddenly realized was one of the heads I'd seen for sale on a specialty website a few months ago. It cost several thousand dollars and his care was well warranted at least out of respect for the price tag. The same man had saved me with a couple thousand bucks for the ones I'd sold him. I was forever grateful for that much, anyway--even if I did and do continue to regret the grudging sale. But, truth be told, I wanted my heads back!

* * *

FORENSIC HEALTH, Court Clinic Program

To: East Boston Criminal Clerks

From: Caitlin R., LICSW

Date: 4/20/16

Mental health evaluation for Mr. John Fay

RELEVANT HISTORY AND CURRENT CIRCUMSTANCES:

(Pertinent excerpts and notable life snapshots --JPF)

John Fay is the eldest of three children born in Malden, MA to his parents Joan and John. He grew up in Milton and then, after the birth of his two younger sisters, the family moved to East Boston. The children were raised in what he described as an educated middle-class neighborhood. From a young age, the defendant was expected to care for his siblings and change their diapers. The defendant described that his father was an alcoholic and was physically abusive towards his mother. The married couple was reportedly "always at each other's throats" and later divorced. His mother was verbally and physically abusive towards him. Per the defendant, Mrs. Fay would "go off her rocker, push me around...she was extraordinarily manic."

He cited instances during which his mother would wake him up in the middle of the night and make him clean the bathroom. A paternal aunt (Ms. Lorraine Licciardi) stepped in and helped raise the children. Although Mr. Fay denied any history of sexual abuse by his parents, he reported that one of his older male cousins was often "sexually aggressive" towards him and his friends. He remarked that, "He'd be coming onto me and my friend...chased me around without his pants on." This behavior began when the defendant was 8 or 9 years old and continued until he was 13 years old.

The defendant reported that he attended the public school systems in Milton and East Boston. He described that he was once placed in a separate classroom "because I was holding my pencil wrong."

In 1997, when he was 20 years old, the defendant joined the Marine Corps and was sent to training on Parris Island in South Carolina. However, according to Mr. Fay, he couldn't pass the required swimming tests. In addition, the naval psychiatrist discovered the defendant's mental health history. Following disenrollment from the military, Mr. Fay would work various kitchen and landscaping jobs, and later owned an online EBay business for 12 years.

Notably, according to Mr. Fay, he once knew a man who let him hold "a real shrunken head". When I questioned him further about this peculiar subject matter, the defendant had what appeared to be a fascination with shrunken heads. He acknowledged that this item is obviously prohibited by law and belongs to an underground black market. Towards the end of the conversation, the defendant seemed to realize that the topic was quite odd and seemed embarrassed by his knowledge of the subject matter.

When Mik handed me the head, an electric surge shot through my whole body. My fingers right up through my arms and into my brain tingled with an electric grace, my heart warmed, and I was as giddy as though I were holding the hand of a new girlfriend for the first time. My friend and Mik stood beside me, seeming to respect my reverence and quietly allowed me a moment to take in what was a profound and rather "heady" experience. The skin was cool and leathery, his hair soft to the touch. The workmanship was wonderful and impressive. I understood the time and commitment it required to successfully shrink a human head. My god, I didn't want to let that thing go. This was on a man's body at one time, I reminded myself with impressed amazement, and as much respect for the dead as I could dredge up, cupping the head in both hands, my fingers partially up inside of the neck hole.

The day was overcast and otherwise dreary, but my mood was lifting by the minute. Hesitant, I returned the tsantsa to Mik, which he locked back up behind the glass of the case. He gave me what I figured was a consolation gift: A MIRACLE OF TAXIDERMY! I didn't leave empty-handed after all…a mummified flying squirrel! I had that poor squirrel right up until my uncle finally managed to throw me out of the windowless bunker apartment, once my aunt died. She had been the buffer between him and me for decades. Ahh … the bunker, where so much sex, fighting, drinking, drugs, and blood had gone down. Now, I want the squirrel back, too.

My alleged future "victim" didn't get a tattooing position there--Mik hadn't been quite impressed enough with his portfolio, apparently. After we left the shop, it occurred to me in the way that everything suddenly makes perfect sense: I would at last try what I'd been mentally romancing for several months by that time. I'd finally take the plunge into heroin. It was what I considered to be the ultimate, end-of-the-line substance of wonderful infamy.

Of course, my friend had the connects, as I was counting on. This is the questionable benefit of surrounding myself with degenerates. This ritual would include my purchasing him a bag too anytime I wanted to "chip." But I didn't mind the junk-head tax. It was standard in this dance of derelicts.

Shawcross was even around for my odyssey of dope, in spirit anyway. I would use one of the shamrock wheels, a four-leaf clover that Shawcross had made encased in a small, transparent plastic wheel, to cut and line up the heroin (or crushed pills, coke, etc.) on my living room table, a dinner plate, or a hooker's stomach--whatever was available. I touched upon my drinking with him but never would've broached the other substances. Especially not the heroin. Shawcross was not a big drinker, apparently preferring to just cut to the chase and strangle people to death. As numbed out as I was keeping myself with one drink or drug, usually in a knowingly deadly combination, I had enough of my mind left to keep the information to myself.

Though, part of me was worried what would happen if I happened to die, as far as Shawcross not knowing why I'd suddenly disappeared. Would he be worried about me? I hoped so, but he was certainly well acquainted with sudden disappearances. Something worth touching upon, though, is I'd made a personal commitment to not die before my bloodline father. There is an instance in my substance abuse history when I literally came back from the dead just so I wouldn't have died before Dad. But other than those two considerations I have been less than concerned about my own death.

Maybe it was the drugs, alcohol, and the general insulation of insanity, but I did feel awkward about leaving him behind like that. In my haze, I thought of writing him into a will of some sort. Although, considering seriously, I didn't know what I could've left him.

Never had I blamed Shawcross for expediting the grotesqueries of the downward trajectories that nearly ended me numerous times. He just happened to be around when my personal hell flared up in earnest. Shawcross was a validating element, though, empowering me the way good fathers do. I was inspired, in a sense, and evermore deeply encouraged by what seemed like a supreme confidence and fuck-it-all embracing acceptance of what he himself was. This, I believed, could apply to all sectors of my own life of fuckery, however wretched, shameful, and streaming with shit.

I was a bit pained that I couldn't join Shawcross. Whatever differences we may have had (for instance, about which cuts of special foods were more appropriate than others--or that eating the more rundown persons of society made for a stringy, rather melancholy meat, in the opinion of some who were allegedly in the know; or not always having the same vision for the approach to the book that he and I were chiseling away at it), we could put those differences aside for the holidays and just, well…be normal. Almost, I daydreamed, a real family. Sure, we were a murderer and a drunk, but I ached for times that didn't entail two divorced excuses for parents bragging about extramarital affairs they'd both had in between passing the stuffing and shoving each other's faces into a dangerously-undercooked turkey.

So, the well wishes from Shawcross and the spirit infused into his letters were the closest I'd had to something like a regular kind of holiday. Although, Thanksgiving does inevitably have a somewhat different tone for the cannibally-inclined.

In my own life, on any given day, I had preferred the ritual of filet mignon or sirloin, cooked so rare that it was practically still breathing, and, to aid the rite, evened out with rum and OxyContin until it all blended into a hue of golden grace, a lifeline from the Divine, chemically manufactured as it was. The drugs and alcohol themselves are sorcery (or pharmakeia, which has Biblical relevance), facilitating the cracking of portals and the parting of otherwise invisible seas. Indeed, dredging demons.

It was a rite of gastronomical transmutation, each bite…

…an ex-girlfriend;

…any girl;

…dead friends;

…my father;

…my mother.

For love, for conquering: imbibing the soul.

Done in my own unique manner, I see it as isolating and tuning-in to certain etheric frequencies to inherit a portion of the visualized peoples' essence. A sorcerer's trick, which I've dabbled with on occasion, but something that I normally keep quiet. Try explaining any of this to your garden variety psychiatrists and the outcome will not be an especially favorable one. You don't have to be a spelling bee champion to spell FUCKED…

The years prior to my drinking, drugging, and downward death roll, I was a sober guy who was disgusted with such brazen acts of self-destruction. Regardless, I did things on a clear mind that underscored something fundamentally wrong with me, at least according to the mores of normal society.

The things I'd done entailed, but were not limited to, shedding and peeling dead skin onto my food to add a certain something, especially to Chinese food. There was, however, no sorcery involved (of which I was conscious, anyway), only a practice that I didn't really understand as I chowed down a generous mountain of mushroom chow yoke, pork friend rice and, of course, human skin.

Later, as I pulled focus on my interest, I purchased some items to serve as, at least, a prop for further enriching my daydreams. A ravioli maker was one of these. I had a thing for meat-filled ravioli and so, playfully (as far I was concerned), I came up with recipes like Catie-filled ravioli (ex-gf and one-time Internet porn girl). On occasion, these tendencies would lead my imagination to get away from me.

01/16/01

Hey John,

I see you found two more Jamaican shrunken heads. They were small to BEGIN with.

Dahmer went to the extremes in PORK CHOPS. He was into dicks, as I was into CUNTS.

Don't you read your mail, John? Or am I just shelved unopened? Even my WIFE has not written. She gets a letter right after this one!

Man, I need a VACATION. I think I'll drive out to your area, pick you up and find a big van with a mattress. Then off to Boston we go and pick up a few and brew. How does that sound, pal? Ready to EXPERIMENT? Mayhaps I could teach you a few pointers. HAHA

One of the women that works here does NOT shave under her arms. HAIRY BITCH! Hits a good 180 LBS AT THAT. All tits and ass but must have one BIG, HAIRY CUNT between there someplace. HAHA

On Friday last I was out in the hallway doing some work and along came a woman with dark red hair and TIGHT pants. MAN, I could see the whole shape of her pussy through her pants. "GOD", I had to turn away or FALL TO MY KNEES!

Some women come here to work don't realize how they look--or they DO and don't give a damn until someone GRABS them! This place is too small for any B.S like of that sort. But some HAVE been grabbed in here. One got fired for jacking a guy off.

She's white and he's black. But she hollers RAPE and the inmate sued her and won! Lots of witnesses, guards and inmates. That woman had to have been 240 LBS at LEAST.

I do have a visit set up for the 26th of January. A woman named Tammy. Kissing and hugging. Maybe dip a finger...or TWO. HAHA Blonde at that. She sent me three cunt hairs. She got some of mine too--a handful of them. HAHA I got a gal that wanted some hair--so I snipped a lock off my head, chest, groin and butt. Wonder what she does with it. Most likely gets off on the thought!

I finished one painting. Working on my last one for the art show. I'll submit ten paintings and one sketch. 500.00 each. Out of that I get $250.00--Crime victims get $250.00. Then I get $125.00 and my wife gets $125.00. A fucking BUMMER, man! Waste of my time. I could make on the eBay. HAHA

Later,

Art

* * *

01//20/01

Hi John,

Your book came in yesterday at noon. Why call this book The 12th Planet? Where are 10 & 11?? Quite interesting! I always knew we came from another solar system!

These photos don't show much. Not that clear. I can

see the outline of a tit through the sweater. She's sure enough PREGNANT. Play with her naval! Tell her she can't have any more sex -- because her child might get a dent in the forehead HA HA! Now, why a photo of a pregnant belly?

You can tell ole Uncle Art. SMiLE

John, I can only get photos of girls with their clothes on. But even a bra and panties will do. I've a few like that. She could flash her tits at me and it wouldn't faze me. "Not the brightest bulb in the tree" was GREAT, man. Really got the laugh going!

Ever screw a deaf mute? Fun, MAN -- Make ALL KINDS OF NOISES, but who can UNDERSTAND??!

In a polar shift, ALL COASTAL CITIES will go under FAST. Upper New York or the mountains of New Hampshire. That area is a safe bet. All around the world will be affected. That blast in Tunguska was atomic in nature. Visitors from outer space crashed somewhere there!

Because Russia did not have a bomb that size. Nor did any anyone ELSE for that matter. An asteroid would have made one HELL of a crater if it had hit. This exploded in the AIR!

You have to remember, that area Siberia was empty of human life. TIME MACHINE PLANTED...There are A LOT of unexplained things going on in the world! Loud BOOMS off the coast of New Jersey down to North Carolina. What was it?

How about an object in the middle of Lake Superior that no one can get to?! The military sent a small submarine in that area and the sub shut down on its own! Divers get disoriented and have to surface. But the investigation still goes on. This summer, the Navy placed a ship above the object and sent a robot down there. Would you believe they lost it? The cable was cut like a hot knife through butter! So now that area is RESTRICTED to ALL SHIPS, BOATS or whatever.

There is MUCH none of us know. But I will bet SOMEONE does!

So a blast that big over a CITY would level it. Every air-breather would DIE instantly!

I'd like to get a stuck-up gal and fuck her everywhere but loose! She'd be a country gal from then on -- dumb and dumber. A too-easy gal is DANGEROUS: Fuck them, AIDS or whatever. Wear Saran Wrap! HA HA

The girl in the photo you sent had nice tits and nipples. Wonder why SHE got killed?! Looks like she had her LEFT TIT CUT OUT. Wasn't ME...this time.

WHO I FUCKED AND WHO I KILLED...

Hair

Blonde -- DARLENE TRIPPIE

Brown -- JUNE STOTTS

Black -- JUNE CICERO

Dark Brown -- DOROTHY BLACKBURN

Blonde -- PATTIE IVES (Cocaine User)

Light Brown -- DOROTHY KELLER (Thief)

Light Brown -- MARIA WELCH

Brown -- ANNA STEPHANS

Black -- ELIZABETH GIBSON

Brown -- PHILESHIA STEVENS (Black woman)

Blonde -- FRANCES BROWN

SHALL I GO ON? GOT YOU THINKING, DO I NOT?

Out of all of them there is only one black chick and one Spanish. The rest are whatever. I AM COOKING LEG OF GIRL -- HAHA. Got my special hot sauce ready.

SPAGHETTI WITH CHUNKS OF "PORK."

Did you know that out of the first eleven there were two Dorothys and two Junes? Strange. FOUR OF THEM LOST THEIR PUSSIES. One only lost her clit.

BAR-B-QUE SPARE SHORT RIBS.

Better stop running off at the lip -- might say something I shouldn't.

Later,

Art

"She's sure enough PREGNANT." This bears some clarification.

The previous Christmas, having lost track of the fact that we were related on my part, I'd taken black-and-white Polaroid shots of my cousin who was eight months pregnant, give or take. I guessed that Shawcross would enjoy a photocopied picture to help illustrate what I'd mentioned about the dear girl. There was a phase when I had, what would probably be deemed unhealthy and decidedly unnatural, a fascination with my first cousin, and, yes, sending photos of her to a serial killer rather did enhance that fascination. Mine was always a sexually dysfunctional family, to acknowledge the least of it. Both of my older female first cousins used to flash me as teenagers when I was still a boy in his single digits. My reaction was more or less bemused, or even indifferent, at the time but, no doubt, it stuck with me, further shaping my perception of sex. As things were, I was already rather precocious with this subject, and, as young as five years old, I began daydreaming of being dominated by women. Although I didn't reasonably comprehend what it was all about, I had no recognizable sense of libido or arousal at the age of five. The out-of-place fantasies were just there, recurring and intrusive. A gathering of women around me as I was strapped down to a leather-bound table was usually the theme.

Before sleep on some nights, these thoughts would sharply enter my mind as I was lying on the very blood-stained mattress I slept on for years, after my father gave me a beating for something for which cousin Michelle had been guilty, while my mother stood by in the brutally uncaring manner to which I never quite adjusted, and certainly never accepted. Something aside from my sexually shady cousins had undoubtedly filtered in. Unless I was simply possessed from the start, overshadowed by an unspeakable ancestral or spiritual lineage.

Nowadays, perhaps ironically, I'm typically sexually conventional. Within reason, of course. Although, certain police reports may seem to indicate differently. But there are many sides to every story. Especially when one can't keep all the variations of his personality in check. And, of course, the blackouts, all the damn blackouts.

So many blackouts…

10/25/01

Hi John,

Let's go check out some AFGHAN WOMEN! Leave the head covered though. AFGHAN pussy is BALD John. Not one hair do they have. Their religion. It's plucked out. "OUCH" KILL ALL THE MEN-- FUCK ALL THE WOMEN--THEN KILL THEM TOO. Anything under 12 gets sent to better homes. Boys over 12 get SHOT! DAMAGED IN THE BRAIN ALREADY. As for the girls...

One has to understand the religion aspect of the Arab. They willingly DIE for their beliefs. Fuck 'em, as you say. By all means possible, anywhere I can... HAHA Mouth, cunt, ass, tits, even up the NOSE!!!!

But why does an Arab down the street get fucked over? What did he do? He is a law abiding citizen and he gets fucked over because of his beliefs. Every man, woman, and child in this country that is not an Indian is from elsewhere. Do we fuck over our neighbors? I'd like to...

HUMAN PIG MEAT. Love it. Makes a tastier bacon! I've eaten it and it's not bad. Definitely not from pigs though. There is a company I think still active on the net that sells human meat.

As it is now, I will start a new program: ALTERNATIVE RESTRICTIVE TRAINING. Deals with violence.

Win the LOTTERY so I can get a good typewriter and ribbons.

Let's see what books I've read this week.

THE FACTS OF DEATH By Raymond Benson

THE DEVIL'S WORKSHOP By Stephen J. CANNELL

NIGHTSHADE By Robert Phillips

THE GROUND BENEATH HER FEET By Salman Rushdie

As you can see, I am into different things. At the moment, I am reading THE INHUMAN CONDITION by Clive Barker.

That sticker you sent was confiscated--Sorry for not saying so.

A nice cool freeze today. Since Friday it's been cool. The heat was on in my cell overnight. Quite a drop from 98 degrees to below 60!

My wife and one grandson are coming on the 10th, our anniversary! On August 3rd there will be a picnic on the big yard for families. I will attend with my wife , daughter, and granddaughter. I ordered my wife a dozen yellow roses. I bet she will be surprised. Seven years of a marriage and I've not got that pussy! As yet, I don't get to use a trailer for a conjugal!

You know John, I'd much rather have 4 wives--Then they would each try the best for my favors! Give me a hundred or so.

I refused to go out to work this morning. We have an ASSHOLE GUARD who is damn lazy! When I need something he won't use the key. So why bother at all? But I will inform the Superintendent in the morning. A guard can write up an inmate but I won't write up a guard. I go right to the top! Then let HIM deal with the fuck!

I did a painting and gave it away to an inmate. I didn't like the end product, so instead of destroying it I gave it away. My first to do so! May not be my last.

But I'll not sign those. I'll try another idea on an 8 ½' x 11" vinyl. I am doing nothing too long! Got to keep busy.

John, if both ice caps melted you'd be living in Ohio now. As for myself, I'll be fucking with someone daily. JUST MY NATURE.

There's some fan club on the West Coast--13 members. Could be a witches' coven.

John, someone is writing letters and claiming they are mine! It's not even my handwriting! Also, someone printed one of my poems and it's all fucked up. I'll fix all those fools! I'll sue and that party gets visited by my BONE CRUSHER... I've a cop who loves to investigate assholes who use me. He has paid a visit to someone out in Illinois. My contact came away with over $500 worth of shit and didn't pay a fucking DIME! Like reaching out and touching someone FOR REAL...GRRRRRR HAHA

Be cool.

Later,

Art

CHAPTER FIVE

I was steadily flirting with something so dangerous it was an unutterably horrible sequence of possibilities.

July of 2001, two months before I'd memorialized Dahmer's birthday on May 21st every year since his murder in 1994), I'd just moved to the bunker flat I rented for a token from my aunt and uncle, and had begun really finding my stride with drinking. The rum, an ambivalent blessing, was internally liberating. The domestic oppression of my liberties had been driving me to plan suicide daily, envisioning my neck on the commuter rail track, and letting the train speeding into Boston answer every prayer of escape from the sprawling lack-of-concentration camp.

The liquor was the reason behind my abrupt and unceremonious eviction from the dollhouse. Leaving my father thirty or so physical miles, and worlds, behind, was the best thing for me. It should've happened sooner, so much sooner, but circumstances had made it impractical. Shawcross was with me throughout the worst of the hell bound rumbling and crumbling, affording me much needed emotional shoring up. A killer pillar in my life, one might say.

As for my father-by-default, at seventeen, in mid-1993, which was my senior year of high school, I informed Father Dumbest, with not an inch left for any doubt, that I would kill him if he ever hit me again. And I meant it. Oh, boy, did I mean it. After he'd been drinking all day, he had punched me in the face in the way a man would do fist fighting with another grown man for no discernible reason other than being a violent, drunken debacle of a human being. Later, trying to explain away the black eye to teachers and classmates was an awkward and embarrassing mess. But with my chemical bomb of emotions, I was finally finding my rage, sense of indignation, and the spirit of hell I'd need to survive and overcome lesser monsters.

It didn't, however, take his hitting me again to be the end game.

Hey BIG BAD JOHN,

Finally got some stamps. A real pain in doing so. Another postage robber on the loose. I keep mine hidden! But if I leave this cell and it opens when I am not here--and something is stolen--I put in a claim for all the stamps bought last. Those guys don't learn, John. You need to CUT the fuckers or BEAT THEM OVER THEIR HEADS. Blacks don't reason-- WHITEY OWES THEM! THIS white guy owes them a HEAD CHOPPING. Cut their dick off and you is a BAAAD DUDE! HAHA

I'd rather look at LIVE bodies--Movement of FLESH. See it SQUIRM some.

John, I can freeze-dry ANY animal or, yes, human quickly and cheaply for however many hundreds of years! Think, John; think of Siberia permafrost. They have tunnels and caves that freeze-dry meat.

COCK-EYED--Right, SURE HAHA: Funny, John, I like it.

Area 51 has my interest. Something tells me that they have machines to hollow out the Earth and put in whatever. Whole CITIES...A LOT of MISSING

PERSONS reported these days: Where do they GO, John? Who would find them if they were taken down THERE?! Wonder how large an object fits into the elevators? John, the only people who work subterranean do not have relatives. ORPHANS: STOLEN KIDS, who knows?!!!!

Yes, a spaceship full of women--ALL colors. THAT way they won't all taste the same. SICK bitches go out the airlocks!

Why is that object in Lake Superior HUSH-HUSH? No one can get near it. WHY?

Scientists are looking for that so-called 12th planet. I've read where one object was spotted past Pluto way out. As yet, they don't know what it is, BUT it's headed in toward THIS fucking system! Check this out, John: Whatever it is, it's HUGE and has no reflection. One of the deep space satellites has been observing it--but so far no word from said satellite. WHY? It's not sending back any information.

I'd like a book on strange, unknown, and unexplained things. I've read another book by Zecharia Sitchin-- GENESIS REVISITED. Not bad. A bit boring though --hits too much on his other book!

In a few days, I'll have some ink sketches ready to ship. Back to pencil drawing again. Can't get ahead at all. I'm working on it. Trust me, John.

Got a letter from my wife today also. Misses me bad. She will be here as soon as the snow melts! I'll close now and get a letter to her

Later,

Art

It was a Sunday afternoon in early fall when I was attempting to help keep whatever tenuous peace there was in the dollhouse by clumsily assisting with yet another unnecessary painting project with which my lost soul, spoiled brat of a mother bullied her way into having us involved. She was usually preoccupied with acting the fool, stumbling after married men at the local restaurant bar like the tramp she didn't become until she was... sixty-years-old!

Unnervingly and forever tense in the claustrophobic little house by the lake (of Fire), there was no escape, privacy, or overall decency coming from anybody. It was an enclosed-setting war with never-ending trauma reinforcements. Now, not particularly knowledgeable about house painting, or skilled in these areas to begin with, I, of course, accidentally knocked over nearly a gallon of paint. A quarter-speed slow-motion spillage of battleship gray paint going everywhere on the pitched roof closed the world in on me and I felt my spirit also spilling right out of my body, floating up and away above the now spectacularly paint-spattered rooftop.

I scrambled, scrabbled, and senselessly babbled, doing anything to wipe as much of the paint up as possible. I was only making it worse, using a rag that was a former face cloth. Good old, and as-per-usual-drunk, Dad ordered me off the roof from where he was now watching me, red-faced and staggering down in the front yard.

"I'M COMING UP TO GET YOU, YOU SON OF A BITCH!" he bellowed, the irony of his having married the bitch clearly going right over the drunkard's dickhead.

For a dragging moment, I was paralyzed, not sure whether I should run--or cover the rest of myself in the paint like Arnold Schwarzenegger with mud in Predator and hope I blended into the spill. Meanwhile, Dad was baboon-climbing the ladder, a bucket in one hand, water sloshing onto his clothes, shoes, and the grass below. Frantic, frenetic, and fast-elevating anxiety, I made at least a show of trying to wipe up the messy spill but was only rubbing it in and smearing it every which way. My father, as soon as he set foot on the roof (he was surprisingly well-balanced for an inebriated jerkoff), snatched the rag, which was dripping gray paint everywhere and covering me from painting cap and coveralls to shoes and socks, out of my hand just to throw it in my face. It seemed like a strangely redundant and grossly counterproductive act to me.

As I made it to the ladder and started climbing down in an effort to avoid further confrontation, Dad dumped the bucket of water he was supposed to have brought up to clean the paint over my head--and the bucket itself soon followed. Again, the counterproductive action seemed pointless. As he often had, he shamelessly made fools of us both in the presence of the neighbors standing around outside, clearly baffled at this sight. All the time, he was doing things like that, embarrassing us all in public, brutalizing our dignity, and thoughtlessly crushing any hope for escape.

Soon, I was thinking that I couldn't do it anymore, that I didn't deserve the barrages of disrespect. I wouldn't take it anymore. My so-called father was some toxic abomination mutation shat out in a spectacular detonation of diarrhea by the Devil's janitor. The Devil would've had the dignity to have killed him at birth, no doubt, like an animal does with any freak of nature it may push out.

That afternoon, I decided to murder my father.

By 1993, two years of quiet mental deterioration after the whispers began making suggestions of undertaking a discreet apocalypse, I was already well into the idea of murder. However, homicide in itself was boring to me. The way I saw it, killing someone was a waste of an otherwise useful body. In general, it wasn't death, though, but a capturing and preserving of an elegant expression of Creation.

But then, on occasion it was all about death. Sometimes, whichever of my moods I happened to have slipped into, I dreamily idealized it as the quickest carpool lane to an ultimately peaceful outcome. Academically referencing, in respectful acknowledgement of the dead who spend their deaths in camouflaged niches and sealed up in cubby holes, there are vast parcels of land and ocean unexplored; undiscovered groves, graves, and nearly bottomless lakes; and abandoned cabins in the misty mountains where an adventurous man can hang his hat and tack up his faces.

The Monday after the family crisis of spilled paint, I began my quest for a firearm. There was a sophomore classmate in Wilmington High who presented himself as having some obscure involvement with criminal types. And so, the bench of prospects as thin as they were, the two of us were walking home Monday afternoon when I took the leap of faith necessary when doing what was essentially a cold call to a superficial acquaintance for buying a weapon that I intended to murder my father with. I casually brought up my interest in locating a pistol.

The weirder part of our otherwise relaxing after-school exchange, as I'd never shared anything about my grossly dysfunctional family life with him or anyone at school, was that he half-jokingly asked, "Why, gonna shoot your father?" No, of course not, I lied, it's only for protection which, like the condoms I picked up a year earlier, I probably wouldn't be using it anytime soon or possibly ever. Promising he'd ask some people whom he had supposedly known, he'd get back to me, he claimed.

All week, into my dreams, I envisioned with elation my father's bullet-shattered corpse at my feet. The only thing I had to look forward to in those days. Then, come Friday afternoon, I got around to asking my friend walking back from school about the gun. But no one whom he knew, he apologetically told me, was carrying or selling guns. It was, I quietly assumed, woefully doubtful that anyone would let me borrow a gun for a night. Disappointed but polite about it, I didn't mention it again. I never got the pistol needed to pursue my dead-daddy dream. The seething was still there, as was the recurring anxiety tremors throughout my body, but I managed to cool down about that particular plan by the end of the week.

Had I still lived in East Boston, however, imagining similar circumstances, as far as motivating events like the spilled paint, I probably would've gotten a gun from the first person I asked. From there, who could know? My sisters have told me since then--confiding in them years later the roughly laid-out plan to kill our father--that they would've testified in my favor and revealed to everyone the abusive nature of our upbringings in the hopes of minimizing the legal outcome for me. However, despite their help, no matter how sympathetic a jury might be, the situation would've led to incarceration of some kind. Even a mental hospital is a prison in its way, except that the "correctional officers" come in pill form. A well-medicated and duly-sedated population is the most ideal jail after all.

But returning to Noddle's Island (aka East Boston) was still the future, just up ahead of me at the very turn-and-burn of the century. Some might say that it was my destiny; others, my doom. Because bloodshed, the odd ritual scarifications, consensual cannibalism, and cocktail party vampirism were the least of my problems.

Hi John,

"Reincarnation…" As long as I don't come back as a woman or a black I'll be ok. Think John on how many people lived in the world way back when! Millions…

I never did ask that question of a victim of who she was when I brought her back. All she asked was: "Who sent you?" Now, why did she ask that? I believe I know where she is coming from or where she was and no more.

The Rogue Warrior was about Navy Seals in their

operations in Europe and other places. The people who are sent that do what normal channels can't, or won't. A lot of words and terms used might not make sense to some but I can follow along ok. The military jargon is easy to follow.

U.F.O.s, I wish one would stop by--I need a lift. Picture that now! I would go in a heartbeat and have them pick up the women...Makes for a smooth ride.

Did you know that where Maria lives there are 26 Shawcross families living there?!

I have a few women I'd like to get close to in one form or another--The next time I'll just shoot them from a quarter mile away! Shoot and move, shoot and move. Never in one spot too long.

About the eBay, your word is always good with me pal.

BIG CAKE with a stripper inside, man, she better be ready for a good long fuck.

Bowlegged when she leaves; if she leaves at all. Two birthday cards came in. One from a blonde from N.Y. and another blonde from Canada.

Knew a blonde woman 6'9" TALL. Blonde all the way. TITS AT LEAST A 44. Pussy was nice too. She (this woman is in my apartment now), Susan, hated people, but loved me in her own way. I went with Susan to see her doctor. What a surprise--ANOTHER female I knew, the doctor. Would you believe I let this doctor park in my parking slot each day? HAHA The doctor asked how I got past her shield. I whispered in her ear. I kissed her pussy and then some! Well, that was a new one on Doc! The DOCTOR was blowing me and I had one of her patients! WILD, don't you agree?!

So, you like the one and only sketch/drawing of me, GRAMPA GHOUL? Cool, don't you think? $30.00 was ok, John. I don't do that stuff much. I'll send some other drawings you can handle.

Keep me posted.

Later,

Art

Looking back, I realized that my biological father could be summed up as the worst of my life's "trolls" or kind of attached-at-the-hip heckler gone violently berserk on vodka and Viagra.

The night I was made by circumstances to move out of the dollhouse--the bad place of crippling sadness where imagination died--marked the seminal moment of my over fifteen years of anarchy in its purest form. Out of control with no controllers; no rulers, and no rules.

Aside from the bucket of water incident on the roof, my father hadn't put his hands on me since seventeen, after the promise that I'd kill him if he ever hit me again. A young man's birth into true adulthood. I was twenty-two the next time it happened. But by then, not only had I zeroed in on my brand of ancient wrath necessary-evil (as-needed hyper-aggression and the serious study of martial arts--particularly, the more practical street combative systems like Jujitsu), but had fortified my dark side with a rising tide of Bacardi mixed rather generously into Hawaiian Punch. It had become the nightly routine: Alcoholic self-hypnosis and obscure horror movies (of which my own life was one) in my oppressive attic room.

He, himself, drunk on that night, Dad barged in with

typical rudeness, complaining about my excessive drinking, which I'd mostly been doing quietly up to then. As he took hold of my wrist, I was able to immediately reverse the circumstances with a day one self-defense trick. Taking a few steps back, the bully shocked by his would-be victim, I threw my glass at him, missing his bulbously-proportioned head by inches, and shattering against the doorframe.

After beating feet out of my sight, he was panicked and tongue-tied when he directed my youngest sister's boyfriend to take me out of there and down to East Boston.

A welcome banishment.

The rabbit wormhole was blasted wide now, opening onto pastures of twilight nirvana lit ambiently by seductively strange suns spotlighting majestic freak shows that most will never even know exist. It all glowed with a subtle vibrancy speaking in satin tones of the purity of untapped odysseys where lust for the odd had no discernible perimeters.

It was becoming clearer why I could bond so seamlessly with Death.

01/20/01

Hi John,

These photo pictures of your cousin don't show much. Not that clear. I can see the outline of tit through the sweater. She sure enough pregnant. "Not the brightest bulb on the Christmas tree" was great, man. Really got a laugh going! Play with her naval. Tell her she can't have any more sex--Because her child might get a dent in the forehead! HAHA Now, why a photo of a pregnant belly? You can tell ole Uncle Art. Smile.

Your book came in yesterday at noon. Quite interesting! Now, why call this book THE 12TH PLANET? Where is ten and eleven?? I always knew we came from another solar system. In a polar shift, ALL COASTAL CITIES WILL GO UNDER FAST. Upper New York or the mountains of New Hampshire are a safe bet. All around the world will be affected. The blast in Tunguska, Siberia, was atomic in nature. Visitors from outer space crashed somewhere there! Because Russia did NOT have a bomb that size-- Nor did ANYONE ELSE for that matter. An asteroid would have made one HELL of a crater if one had hit. This exploded in the AIR! You have to remember, that area was empty of human life. TIME MACHINE PLANTED...A blast that big over a city would LEVEL it. Every air-breather would die instantly!

There are a LOT of unexplained things going on in this world! Loud booms off the coast of New Jersey down to North Carolina. What made them?

How about an object in the middle of Lake Superior that no one can get to?! The military sent a small sub down there and it shut down on its own! Divers get disoriented and are forced to surface. But the investigation still goes on. This past summer the Navy placed a ship above it and sent down a robot. Would you believe they LOST the robot?! The cable was CUT like a hot knife through butter! So now that area is restricted to all ships, boats, or whatever.

There is MUCH none of us knows. But I will SOMEONE does!

John--I can only get photos of girls with their clothes on. But even a bra and panties will do. I've a few like that. She can flash her tits and it wouldn't faze me.

Ever screw a deaf mute? FUN, man! Make all kinds of noises but who can UNDERSTAND?!

I'd like to get a stuck-up gal and fuck her everywhere but loose! She'd be a country gal from then on--DUMB AND DUMBER. A too easy gal is DANGEROUS--AIDS or whatever. Fuck them with Seran wrap, HAHA

The girl in that other photo had nice tits + nipples. Wonder why she got killed?! Looks like she had her left tit cut out.

I am cooking LEG OF GIRL--HAHA Got my special hot sauce ready. Spaghetti with chunks of "pork."

The list following the first set of names--Seven are dead. Out of all of them there is only one black chick and one Spanish. The rest are...whatever. Did you know out of the first eleven there were two Dorothys and two Junes: Strange. FOUR of them lost their pussies. One only lost her clit. BAR-B-QUE SPARE SHORT RIBS.

"Hair"

Blonde--Darlene Trippie

Brown--June Stotts

Black--June Cicero

Dark Brown--Dorothy Blackburn

Blonde--Patti Ives

Light brown--Dorothy Keller

Light brown--Maria Welch

Brown--Anne Steffen

Black--Elizabeth Gibson

Brown--Phileshia Stevens (black)

Blonde--Frances Brown

Shall I go on? Got YOU thinking, do I not? Who I fucked and who I killed...

"Hair"

Blonde--Barbara Dobson

Blonde--Karen Hill

Redhead--Kathy Murdock

Brown--Mildred Winters

Blonde--Colleen Lund

Brown--Nancy Salisbury

Brown--Martha Carr

Brown--Sarah Chatterson

Blonde--Linda Neary

Black--Penelope Shabino

Blonde--Irene Kane

Blonde--Sillia Rositer

Black--Susan Rigestagna

Brown--Rose Stilson

Blonde--Darlene Walley

Blonde--Laura Anderson

Blonde--Jack Blake

Brown--Michael Miller

Brown--David Edson

Brown--Kim-Su-Yong

Blonde--Darlene Sawyer

Blonde--Beverly Horning

Blonde--Sheron Van Dewalker

Black--Laura White

Brown--Kara Duda

Blonde--Kimberly Sanderson

  Better stop running off at the lip--Might say something I shouldn't.

Later,

Art

Nineteen was the first and only time I paid for any kind of sex (as of this writing, of course, one never knows) when a thirty-year-old Brazilian friend of mine from work set it up. According to him, the lovely woman had approached him in the rear parking lot of the donut shop when he was out on a smoke break. Later on, and after a few beers, I ended up in the passenger seat of her car. She was nice enough and we got along fine on a surface level, but I found it to be an awkwardly loveless and clinically stainless steel encounter. Although the concept itself was intriguing and had the black-market appeal to which I'd always been attracted.

I wouldn't come across another woman renting herself out until I was twenty-four. But it wasn't for anything especially sexual. At the time, I had considered taking her head home with me. Not that it was a particularly pretty head. She was a little rough around the edges and no frills, but beggars can't be choosers.

A few nights before going out to test the waters, there was a lady in her late thirties, who I caught sight of, offering her services (rather sloppily, as she clearly had an untenable drug problem--and it does take one to know one) to passersby in East Boston's Day Square, when my uncle and I were driving by on our way back from a random errand. An unusual thing for East Boston to be happening right out in the open. Seeing her out there got certain wheels turning, far removed from simple sex.

The week leading up to my excursion was laced with fistfuls of Ativan, anti-anxiety medication I'd gotten a hold of from my aunt, which was the closest semblance to food taken with the escalating rum cocktails. The Ativan and rum dramatically magnified the funhouse that was my mind. Finally, on my own, indeed, I wanted to explore everything that was available. One night, I had the idea to take a trip, anywhere, using the American Express gold card that Auntie Ativan had secured with my name on it, but on which she was billed. She was trying to overcompensate oftentimes for the mother I'd really missed out on. That led to some retrospectively warped overcompensations at some points-- such as, when I got to insisting on it, renting adult films for me way before I was old enough to take them out myself (or to be aware why I was even watching them, for that matter). Though, porn was fairly ubiquitous around her home anyway. Uncle, for example, had a lifetime subscription to Hustler magazine and issues were left out on the living room coffee table. It was a passive, somewhat indirect sexual education, and nothing was forced. In Auntie and Uncle's defense, they were drunk and stoned on hashish most of the time.

So, with my brand-new card, a pocket of Ativan, and no definite plan, on a whim, I purchased a Greyhound ticket to New York City. Several hours later, the alcohol wearing off and not having had the foresight to pack up more rum (it was still early into my addictions and I was not yet the consummate professional degenerate I later became, but I was getting there), the two-a.m. bus out of Boston's South Station pulled into Manhattan as the day was breaking. By then, my interest in this random trip was wearing off. Still in a part-stupor, I wandered the Port Authority Bus Terminal to pass the time until the bus back to Boston pulled in. During those couple of hours, I witnessed at least a dozen New York prostitutes strolling about and one pimp obstinately denigrating his "employee" as he was poking her in the face with a giant glass crack pipe. Evidently, according to the pimp linguist's smattering of "Dumb junkie HO!" punctuations, drugs were interfering with this hooker's enviable Manhattan career. If ever there were a reason for me to stay clean, that wasn't it. There was too much happening there all at once, and I, in no sense, felt like I could have an extended settlement over there. In a flash of clarity, I recalled that Shawcross was right upstate from me and I did have the credit card, but that panicky feeling was creeping up again.

I had to get back to the bunker. Even the anti-anxiety medication didn't help all that much with the generalized angst. It would've been immeasurably worse had I any idea of the terror event coming down the pike two months from when I'd traveled to Manhattan on a seeming drunken whim. It was, however, bad enough. In a place where I had no family or friends there was a kind of comfort that at least came with knowing that Arthur was under the same New York sky that July morning.

East Boston and its sidewalks of desiccated gum and Dave the moldering bum, corrupted in its own familiar way, was a more intimate setting. It was part of who I was. Raised on local accounts of bodies discovered inside the trunks of abandoned cars under the bridge adjacent to Santarpio's Pizza. And, of course, what child could forget the cautionary tale of the young man unable or unwilling to repay his debts to alleged mob figures and his corpse, minus the heart, was left very indelicately in the driveway of his parents' home three houses away from where I lived for the first five years of my life. Most children are warned to look both ways before crossing the street, but we were warned it might be better to not cross the street at all, ever. Jodie, a family friend, was viciously stabbed to death next door to my paternal grandparents' home in Eastie, having apparently spurned a local man after a party. The same murderer was, at the beginning of the detectives' inquiry, luxuriating in a lounge chair on the sidewalk outside of the woman's place, pretending to want to assist with the investigation. Yet another time, a guy in the next house over to Jodi's beat his stepfather to death with a claw hammer. These things happen.

But then, there was Linda.

Linda was once a tenant of my aunt's. I remember her being thirty-seven and me being a relatively naïve eighteen, her having a clear interest in arranging a tryst. But I was too standoffish during my fledgling early adulthood. However, I'd written into a novella a character based on Linda who had her skull cracked apart. In the story, she was dismembered, stuffed into a garbage bag and carried back to the house of the killer's father in the dad's car without the witless parent's awareness of what was in the absurdly oversized green plastic bag.

Years afterward, I would find myself feeling guilty after her new husband in their new house took a new sledgehammer and crushed Linda's head as she lay sleeping in her bed. Then he did likewise to Linda's teenage son, Michael, before walking down to the basement and hanging himself. Adding to the literally and figuratively mind-blowing element, the tenant who moved into the apartment that she'd rented from my aunt was the person working for the funeral parlor who retrieved Linda's body. At the wake, out in the hallway, my uncle pulled the kid aside and asked curiously how much of a mess she'd been before they fixed her up with a wig for the open casket in the next room--in head-to-head caskets with Michael, whose head was "repaired" with a ski cap. Oh, yes, a mess, indeed…Standing there before the pair of open caskets, I flashed on the scenes written by me. Not a subscriber to coincidence, I wondered if I'd somehow either tapped into prophecy or, perhaps, through a terrifying twist on manifesting what one focuses on, it was some quantum physics accident I caused. It's a discomforting thought when standing and then kneeling to make the sign of the Cross (despite not being the Roman Catholic I was raised as anymore, but when in Rome…), before such an already surreal sight. I didn't dwell. Though, I couldn't forget, either.

People don't get much deader than that mother and son were. Friends once, now lying in head-to-head caskets. No reason for why it happened was ever given. It made the tragedy even more mysterious to me. Shawcross came up with apparent motivations for his own murders, they were sexual in nature for whatever that might be worth, but here was a man who'd picked up a sledgehammer, apparently out of the blue, and pulled a Gallagher watermelon trick on his family. The youngest daughter, Jenny, found the body of her mother before running back outside screaming, "My mother, my mother!" Had she been home that night, she too would've gotten the melon treatment from this guy that none of us liked to begin with. He was the reason my aunt and uncle made the family move out of the apartment. Then, practically overnight, there stood poor Jenny in a far-off corner of the funeral parlor tightly clutching a teddy bear to herself, staring off into nothingness. Obviously, the trauma of the gruesome scene (bedrooms walls decorated with skull fragments, bits of brain, and lots of blood) had virtually demolished her. None of us had gotten good vibes from this particular killer. However, Linda was a lonely woman and maybe too eager for another marriage and a financial buffer. Why I envisioned Linda's character having her head bludgeoned, who knows? But it gives me the creeps. Writing can and does take unexpected turns, and there are times when the lines do blur--or disappear altogether.

It's been the same with life, though.

02-01-01

Hey Big Bad John,

How's it kicking, man? I am somewhat OK. Took a fall but bounced back up. But not quite as fast! Stepped in a few spots of baby oil one of the jigs spilled. Quite knocked the wind out of me! I took a long hot shower and two muscle relaxers; then bed. I feel good!

I sent a letter to a woman in Austria who loves to be whipped, spanked, and cursed at before and during sex. As a teenager, she claimed to FUCK DOGS. Wanted a puppy I bet. HAHA Now THERE is a woman I'd love to play with and told her so! At least she can't have any more kids! This woman loves to be tied up tight: MAN, she met the guy who can DO it.

Have you heard of the Rex that lived in the Mexico area? Bigger than T-Rex? DAMN: RED ALERT!

We have a THIEF in the unit. One of the white guys lost the stamps he just bought. Someone is going to be hurt bad. This guy places a mark on all his stuff. So, the mailman will be on the lookout for a stamp from this unit. Each unit has its own mailbag. So there is not that much to check out. If I see ANYONE going into my cell, he will live there and become my BITCH!

Some of these guys have nothing--but to steal here is BAD!!!

Nine paintings and one sketch ready to go. My projection is to have over half sold--or ALL!

If a stamp cost $10.00 EACH, I QUIT! When water costs $20 a quart, the world will END!

What do I call a female hitchhiker? MINE: Smile

The redhead is in the hallway daily. Now I see another chubby one that is busted out from the cunt area. So why wear white pants?! For SHOW AND TELL!

Tell me, John, what did women shave their backs with back in ancient Rome? A BROAD SWORD! HAHA Plucked them out! Some island tribes in the early days used clam shells to take off the pussy hair. After a while, it didn't grow back; nor did their kids have any.

I am eating a lettuce sandwich with tartar sauce. RABBIT FOOD. I have a small pile of snow in my cell. One of the guys got a big bag of snow to cool off my ice box. I've seen guys argue over ice--I use snow. There's plenty of that outside!

Have you ever heard the expression--Grass clippings off the playground? I sent a gal some nut hair. HAHA Well, I better shut down. Take care now.

Later,

Art

A week after my impromptu trip to Manhattan, I was again fueling myself with rum and anti-anxiety meds when I was compelled to see if, out of curiosity, I could track down the Day Square hooker. I wasn't sure what I was expecting but doing so would be another notch in fleshing out some exceedingly damnable ideas. More to further feed fantasies than to act anything out. Then again, life was proving more and more unpredictable. Thoughts like these are usually not shared anywhere but in rooms tucked away behind book cases on some private estate somewhere that doesn't officially exist.

In the presumable off chance that I did come across the woman, I took the "just in case" next step of carrying a plastic shopping bag, shoved into my pants pocket. I wasn't as sophisticated yet as to wearing a backpack, in which to this day I imagine carrying around a head. Past two a.m., I was alternately relaxed and with butterflies as I strolled through the streets that July 13, giddy, terrified, and feeling such terrible enchantment. While I looked for her endlessly, mostly, I hoped not to find her. The most gruesomely off-beat part of the fantasy had me carrying the woman's crackhead back to the bunker with me in that cheap shopping bag. At best, a crude outline of a disorganized plan.

An hour into my flirt with hunting, I decided to go back home with nothing to justify my jangled nerves except the eeriness of the streets during those hours, the orange glow of the street lamps coloring my living dream. I was quickly beginning to realize it might be preferable for everyone to find my heads in a manner that wouldn't cause me instant eligibility for a thousand years in a subterranean concrete tomb for the living dead. The question persists for me to this day, what would've happened if I had run into the woman. Virtually surrounded by butchers and acts of butchery, my answers are probably not far off.

02/17/01

Hey John,

I may be late in getting back to you but, sooner or later, I'll get to it.

On Wednesday last, I went to the library and what do I find? The same book you sent--The 12th Planet. Hey, where might 10 + 11 be about NOW? If there is a 12th planet that we've not seen or heard of, no one can live on it! Pluto is damn cold and frozen.

The asteroid belt has some merit in that something blew up. Did we come from Mars?? NOT ME. I came from way beyond our solar system. HAHA

I've inquired about more information on that object in Lake Superior and, for some reason, it's HUSHED UP! Why? Something is not being told to us!!!!

"Chupacabra" you mention--"GOAT SUCKER" HAHA I know some COCKSUCKERS! HAHA

What is under Area 51? Did you know that there are over 20 stories going down into the Earth there? Little pieces of the puzzle I pick up.

Give me a spaceship filled with girls and women and I'll get busy--Want a lift, John? Some would be strapped down and some just strapped. But all would be healthy! It goes without saying that any with DISEASE will DIE! A stuck-up chick would be one FUCKED UP BITCH when I got done with her! Any chick can be picked up, John. Depends on the method doing so. DART them to sleep. What a wakeup: "DINNER"

I've seen pregnant bellies and pussy quite a few times. So, you like my dent in forehead comment? HAHA What did you tell your cousin?

John, I can't paint anything very bizarre. Not allowed here. Will try out something for you.

I'd be one healthy M.F. in a plane crash. Toasted is nice, HAHA! CLIT STEW--Man, I like your joke, COOL! You'd need A HUNDRED to get a bowl full! I'll use your joke with one of my blondes. Hey, when you beat a gal badly, you're really applying tenderizer before baking. HAHA Raw pussy is only edible frozen. Fresh cut is greasy! Dried is nice too!

I remember all my women, John. Two Dorothys and two Junes is unheard of. Wonder what the odds are or were on that?!

A head could be freeze-dried. Flash frozen: Set in a display case so no air gets to it. Just like the day taken!

Hey John, I do not chop off blonde and red heads. I want them ALIVE and JUICY. We can ALWAYS lop off BUM HEADS.

What I'd like to do with gays who pretend to be gals I'd shove through a wood chipper. One piece at a time. Cut off a leg or arm while still alive so they can see it ground up. What a trip that would be!

Check the net for "MUSEUM OF DEATH." Some woman on "Ripley's Believe it or Not" had or has a letter from every serial killer in the country. Not from ME has she got one!

My pal found the stamp thief. What that fool did not know is that all the stamps had a dot on them. The fool still had the whole roll. Guess what happened next?! He never had time to cry out. He will have a sore throat and an almost busted head--It got stepped on by a 354-lb man.

I'll close for now. Time to wash up.

Later,

Art

It has been said that when a student is ready the teacher

will appear. For some of us our teachers are brutal sadists and sexual deviants, and the lessons are taught in very peculiar ways.

The shade of a tree, however, doesn't diminish a tree's value, only complements it.

As for finding "normal" women, it's never easy, under the most Starbucks-ideal of situations, to partner up with anyone and make some kind of satisfying existence with the person. It's exponentially complicated by personal demons, and having mad butchers like Arthur Shawcross-- additional to a melting pot of other miscellaneous maniacs-- as sub-rosa residents in my life. And then, I also have a deep reticence toward any kind of commitment at all to begin with. Hookers have somehow crossed my path several times, though not overall as a result of lurking for sexual luxuries. While my sister was living in one of the more disparate local motels, she made several prostitute friends and we all would occasionally hang out together to do drugs together or my sister would be chauffeuring one around town to meet a client and I'd break up my day by tagging along. Then I met a girl at a job who asked me out leading me to believe my female dry spell was finally over, and she too ended up being a hooker. This I didn't find out until I'd already bought us, along with an escort friend of hers, a hundred dollars in crack and another hundred in drinks. The friend of hers I figured out pretty quickly what she was doing, as we all strolled the streets of Chelsea together and she'd continually jump into cars or practically drag men into back alleys. But I have to admit that I did a double and then a triple-take when my "girlfriend" started to pull tricks herself. I might've been the only male in Chelsea that night who didn't get to have sex with my date. It is a rare breed, of which I am one, who can spend hundreds of dollars on two hookers in one night and manage to avoid sex altogether.

Throughout it all, the darker side of it all is that it's hard not to have flashes of "What would Shawcross do?" spiraling through my mind sometimes.

And of course, as it turned out, my fear of commitment was justified right to the hilt. They did eventually, after all, have me committed.

CHAPTER SIX

Aztec royalty had a preference for the palms of their sacrificial victims. Apparently, it was a delicacy among the cannibal higher-ups. As I see it, this is an interesting corkscrew twist on the concept of Palm Sunday. Imagining the most obscene rebellion against an often-confusing Roman Catholic upbringing, I dreamed up celebrating Palm Sundays with a full day's diet of human palms. Even a breakfast of palm pancakes, and I don't usually eat breakfast.

The Shawcross diet consisted of other portions of the anatomy but, on that, he and I differed. A "bone of contention," some might discern between us. I leaned more toward the palates of the Aztec elite.

Surreal, everything then. Date and time, abstract, creating a kind of ethereal un-reality as the volume of madness was boosted. Life was coming rapid-fire, days compressed into moments as my death-defying indulgences went full-blown. Alcohol, drugs, shrunken heads, and Shawcross were one continuous psychedelic blur with a fading and re-emerging soundtrack like a metropolis of tortured souls playing in a loop just under the rumbling voice of Shawcross reminding me to "Be good or good at it."

GREETINGS BROTHER,

Hey, John. How's life with you been? Last evening some pussy got creamed over two bluffs and along a highway in Colorado. Trying to land a private jet in a snowstorm! A pilot from California can't fly in snow. Not ANYMORE, that is.

Wish I was at the "landing" site first! 18 people were in the plane--So you've got to figure at least 7 to 8 cunts. Picture getting a BLOWJOB and you CRASH...OUCH! HAHA Now there would be a "cock-eyed" joke for REAL!!!!

Great on the book HANNIBAL. How do you feed brain oatmeal to yourself? Drill a hole, insert straw and get to sucking--Oh, what a RUSH...

I'd sure like to get a hold of some Arab girls. They have no hair on their bodies from the neck down. SAVES SHAVING BEFORE THE SKILLET (as you were so concerned about that bit of food prep--no need to thank me). Smile

NO, John, you don't cook pussy alive. The blood has to be drained. You're welcome.

Chicken hearts become tender boiled slowly for 2 ½ to 3 hours. Same as ANY meat. Add onions diced up--Add pepper only.

A natural freezer in East Siberia, Russia. Permafrost goes deep!

Those other books you mentioned are what we both like: Anything unexplained, supernatural, BIZARRE...Like ME.

By the way, John, I put my stamps in a cleaned-out can of Hershey's cocoa. One can is dark brown and plastic. Like chocolate! If it ever comes up again, someone will have to get a NEW ASSHOLE!!!! I'll cut that motherfucker across the back of both hands!

When my art re-supply gets in, I'll do some inks and ship them off to you.

LOTTERY, cool: 14-26-38

This Sunday, April Fool's Day. I'll call my wife. I should not get too far in joking with her--she might not appreciate our humor. John, I've got other guys' wives who portray their love to me! I keep asking for a visit to PROVE it. Got to ask if you want to know for sure!

Off to work I go.

11:46 AM. Back from work. For the count and lunch. The unicycle alien picture you included looks like she inserted the whole seat! OUCH! I'll see about doing a U.F.O. drawing for you when some stuff comes in, ok, pal?

John, that guy under the bed, where was his head when found? In a case like that it had to be a pimp or homosexual. Cut his head off to suck his own dick. A good lesson on his partner! HAHA I'm sick.

You can address to me like this if you want:

ARTHUR J. SHAWCROSS

91B0193

P.O. BOX 116

FALLSBURG, N.Y. 12733-0116

You don't need to put the prison on it.

Charlie Manson did not kill anyone, true! But his influence has others do his bidding. If he were let go, at any time in his life, he'd have many flock to him again...

The cops have been fucking with me again. Now I am informed that they think I've killed 19 prostitutes. See, how nice. I HAVE KILLED MORE THAN A MERE 19 PEOPLE!!!

It seems that the city of Rochester, New York has murders they can't solve. I bet if they really look at one of their own they will find the guy that did it! Copy cat on me!!!!

This morning I went out to the large recreation yard to get some sun and walk. Quite nice out there. In the 70s. Clear skies at that. This afternoon I'll go back out to watch a football game or two. Maybe read a book or bullshit with the younger set. This evening I'll stay in and paint. Busy day. I keep busy at something. Tried to call the wife but that phone of hers is still blocked--SOMEONE has to pay the phone bill! It will stay turned off until the middle son pays it.

Man, I feel like shit. Coughing, sneezing, but I've started to sweat and that is a good sign.

Damn, there goes the bell. Time to shut down for the night.

6:02 AM. Coffee is on and the aroma is a real wake up! Oh, that tastes good. Spanish dark coffee. Strong and black. All I need now is a gal for 24 hours. HAHA I would be bowlegged and whipped. SHE would be...

On my radio I am playing classical music. It is soothing. I could listen to this all day as long as it's turned low.

Someone is selling tattoo flash of mine. WHO? It is

either out of Florida or Westchester, N.Y.

I need to shave, wash up, and put on my clothes for the day ahead.

Take care, John. Write when you can. Thanks again.

Later,

Art

Some friends talk politics and sports, debating the finer points of whatever happens to be in the mainstream trough on any given day. Shawcross and I discussed the inconvenience of ill-timed body discoveries, human edibles, and my preferences in chemical numbing agents for personal insulation from inner and outer horrors.

Life comes in many strains of hazes when drinking, snorting coke and OxyContin, and blanketing oneself with death and representations thereof on a daily basis. The gods always do punish us, at some point. But until then, we go about the business of catastrophe creation, of self and every living thing within the immediate radius. The only ones who got a pass in those days of destruction were the cats my aunt and I were raising. We had shelters for them in the backyard and a heated garage (that is, until my uncle closed it off after Auntie Lorraine passed away, causing most of the cats to wander off and die). The cats were the only reason I hadn't gone and been a suicide for the period I was living and dying in the bunker. Cats, drugs, and rum kept my mood bolstered and the metaphorical gun holstered as I fluctuated between debilitating depressions and periods of wilding generally unheard of in any civilized society. That tucked away place was turned into a consensually arranged abattoir of drug-inspired oddities and sexual freedoms that occasionally woke my aunt sleeping just above us in her apartment. Admittedly, it was embarrassing when Auntie drunkenly tried to mimic the moans of the girl she happened to hear the night before to let me know in her own way that we were all keeping her awake. "Dysfunctional" is too kind for said family.

What was most frustrating and unfortunate was that in certain cases it wasn't even me involved with the sexual episodes, but my blood brother, best friend Mike. Indeed, the same one who later stabbed me and left me for dead, and the same one I allegedly stabbed back a couple years later, for which I spent ten days in jail, before the case was finally dismissed. Mike would shack up with one of his two girlfriends in my bathroom/laundry room where I had a TV and VHS player set up, play porn, shoot dope, and make bitter love with girlfriend #1 or #2, as I did my best to block it out, sniffing line after line of painkillers or any other available sniffables. No worries, though. My aunt got to walk in on my girlfriend, "Restraining Order Alyssa," and me at least three times while we were together and Auntie was trying to do one of her dreaded unannounced pop-ins. Thankfully, I was so drunk during those times that I hardly noticed or cared. It was Alyssa who alerted me to it. What could I have done, anyway? Auntie had already seen me very naked several times, passed out at her doorstep or in the bunker. She'd been a nurse at one time, I reasoned, so she was relatively used to such things. Plus, she was usually drunk herself. It worked out for everyone--except when she called ambulances for me and I'd wake up in the hallway of the Emergency Department of Mass General Hospital or in the back of one of the ambulances on the way there and punch one of the EMTs in the face. Then, of course, it was four-point restraint city. Those predicaments are quite challenging to talk one's way out of.

Suffice it to say, my home has been a special domain where inhibitions are left at the door with your shoes--and pants (and, actually, the shoes can stay on); and imagination is the name of the game.

Throughout all of this, and despite the unbridled

depravity, I always made sure to feed the cats. The four indoor cats living with me would surround me oftentimes while I was passed out in the bunker somewhere. One of them would even lay down across my liver, which is something he otherwise never did, as if he sensed that I was in desperate need to of healing.

It had to be pointed out by one of my caseworkers that my adoration of cats didn't necessarily mean I had a "softer" side because, after all, cats are serial killers in their own way too. So much for redemption.

Still, I kept the suicide dream alive, scouting around for the perfect tree from which to noose myself dead in a worst-case scenario situation. And of course, every day was some version of a worst-case scenario. This would go on for years, until I found the tree.

Hello John,

You need to laugh. Bad mood swings I noticed with you.

Thanks for the money order: When I got to the store there was $12.12 in there for me. Without your M.O. I have NOTHING.

Yesterday at work while working on a machine I sprayed my hands with WD-40 to rub on some cables and I found that later most of the pain in my hands was gone! WD-40 loosens joints for real! Whether it's a bolt, screw, human hands, or whatever, it works!

Someone in this unit has messed with the clock hanging off from upstairs. Now, my watch says 7:22 AM, but the clock has 7:04 AM. We now have a standing count at 7 AM, 11 AM, AND 5 PM. All because one man died and the guards weren't doing their jobs!

Today is my wife's birthday. She is 70. No more will she be doing the 69. HAHA

John, I got a whisper that a female who writes me is a MALE. So, I stopped writing to all except the one I know PERSONALLY - VISITED: Fingered too. HAHA

Last night I was given a pound and a half of corned beef. Spaghetti tonight. I do know that some roast beef butt ends are coming, plus flour, baking powder, sugar and spices

When I go into work this morning I'll spray my knuckles with WD-40. Left hand is a bit sore.

3 Japs in a restaurant beating off at their table and the waitress SCREAMS at them, "WHY ARE YOU DOING THAT HERE??" One Jap says, "Lady, menu says, 'FIRST COME, FIRST SERVED '..." Your joke of the day, pal.

Take it easy,

Art

As any echoes of rationality got fainter and further away at a now interminably quickened rate, I replied to Shawcross under the vice-grip spell of cocaine and alcohol far more often than not. Occasionally, consulting with one of my mummified heads for advice--or inviting whatever outside spiritual forces willing to work through me to get past an ordeal of writer's block or planning the next gray-area hustle for added income. Like anything I wrote, even in my most inebriated days, the music of the word is sacred. Besides that, I was always conscious that I was dealing with someone I could easily offend and, consequently, lose. Almost like the cats I kept, a misstep due to some momentary mental malwiring might bring about disastrous consequences. So, I had to be on point, regardless of what mountain of shit I was pinned under.

One constant about my life with Shawcross was that he did make the weird twists and turns not feel as horrible to harbor, even normal, in the sense that it was normal--for us, the morbid minority. Although cozy and comforting, it often slipped my mind that these things were scary, even terrifying, for the mainstream. By the time I had second thoughts about letting Alyssa see things that were better left unseen, allowing her to peek into Art's and my world, I was reading about just how big a mistake it'd been in her police statement from April of 2011.

If I had attempted to kill her, as was alleged, I didn't honestly recall. Yet, I don't vehemently deny it, either. Probably, it is true because it is something that has historically happened whenever I got too close with people in any relationship (men, women, and at least one transvestite). Not that I was even consciously trying to hurt any of them. Things just got weird in very surreal ways when the enchantment came, certain people appearing to me framed by seductive, liquid auras of gracefully snaking brooks of deep red and near-black blood. As for strangulation, there was a time when randomly I'd, indeed, lock a chokehold on a friend for a few seconds, getting a wrathful rush, and blanketing me with a feeling of being especially close to the person. If I did try to strangle my girlfriend, it was likely my over-exuberantly expressive affection. Or, possibly, it was as simple as Alyssa ordering the "wrong type of Chinese takeout" and me taking far too seriously egg rolls vs. spring rolls. And why not? One thing about Chinese food is that it was here for me long after she was gone with the wind. Strangulation, however, and/or a twelve-inch knife to the throat might've been a blackout-drunk over-reaching of trying to make a point about the nuances of how to properly order Chinese food, even in my opinion.

Some of us are extremists in our antisocial skills.

Days passed seamlessly and strangely as the Shawcross correspondence piled up in the bunker. The gradual annihilation of my life was in full effect. A convicted cannibal killer in the periphery, a gory canvas of the bloody punctuations of self-mutilations, and puked up pork fried rice on the walls, ceiling, and, far more often than not, dried to a hard crust in every hair on my body. The stale taste of vomit in my mouth, I read one of the letters, hoping to ease the sense that the universe was mortified about the obscenity of the lifestyle I was leading, oscillating and morphing nearer to a death-style all the time. A desperate reach for something comforting. Generally, Shawcross still never made me regret my eccentric ways, even as family members abandoned me along with all but the most intensively offbeat friends (and they were not many). But now, it was all incongruous and nothing as ordered as it had been in the beginning of our exchanges. I was sleeping with the letters under my pillow, strewn all over and under my bed, and, for whatever reason, tucked inside of cereal boxes. Sometimes I'd reach for a letter as I crawled up out of a nightmare. I just needed to be reminded that I had an ally out there somewhere. But days and dates meant nothing anymore. Even the sky appeared differently, like a computer-generated image of macabre fluorescence; a living aura of devilish energies I'd notice on a mission to any liquor store which had not banned me just yet. Even the smells were different and bizarre. The air carried an evil, otherworldly chemical odor, and I sensed strongly it was something that someone smells right before death--if he were to die with exceptional violence. The eBay business I operated for several years was coming apart because of the disintegration of my time perception. Time: it's a Saturnian construct anyway, I dizzily reasoned, and Saturn represents restriction. Who needs it?

Still, try to explain that to customers who haven't received their packages in more than two months. There were more occasions of damage control and, if I didn't mosey around to addressing their complaints, negative feedback started to show up for the first time. A seriously precarious balancing act but I also applied that damage control to my dealings with Shawcross. Even if some of the things I discussed were on the random end of insanity, such as women with horses-- in unnatural ways--extraterrestrials and more obscure issues with Chinese food; jumping from asking how his Easter was right into mummified heads and butchering hitchhikers.

Hi John,

I have THE SILENCE OF THE LAMBS in our library. Better than HANNIBAL by a LONG shot! The author made a LOVE STORY out of it. But a FORCED love story using drugs. Another sequel may be written yet! John, on average I read about ten books a week, sometimes more--depends on the book. There are a bit over 9,000 books in our library and I've read over half of them. 4,000 or more. The librarian claims I have read more books than anyone who has come in. What is cool, he'll ask about each book too. Show me the cover and I'll give you a rundown on its contents. But check this out, John--those 4,000 are only in Sullivan. I'd say I've read maybe 12,000 books in my lifetime. I've read every "Louis L'amour" Western! Owned them all. The FBI took my collection.

John, as a teenager I had a telescope and I looked at the stars at night. Some things I've seen had no meaning to me. Like, "What was THAT?!" I know in my heart and soul that intelligent beings are on the Earth somewhere!

A ghost is nothing more than a spirit left behind on this side. Picture ME as a ghost: I'd lift a lot of dresses, skirts and shirts. Get fucked by a ghost.

HAHA Invisible Man...

HEY NOW--How can a woman get a HORSE COCK in her MOUTH??? Where DO you find this information?!

Chinese food can't go to waste!

I came across an accident that bad like the one your EMT father saw, the guy with no head. Five women drunk inside and outside the car. This was the turnpike in California. I chomped on each one and fucked them all, plus took them to my apartment. Big fun for the wife and neighbor. When sober they asked about their car. I had it outside next to mine. Their car rolled over a few times and was on its side when I got there. Easy to push onto its wheels, tow it out, and home. I had a tow bar on my car. When all was going ok, I was invited to a club downtown. Free of charge for anything I wanted. John--that meant any girl there! DID I? You bet your ass I did. Took a while. I went home late. Couldn't get it up for shit. But I did take a shower before going home. HAHA

You have NO CAR?! "SHAME!" Now, I would have got that gal you saw. Carry a TAZER--"ZAP". HAHA She'd wake up WELL FUCKED, MAN!

Hitchhiking does have its drawbacks. When I was 15 I hitchhiked home from school. Got a ride and a BLOWJOB as well. Plus I got that fool's wallet. He was drunk. My cousin Ronny and his brother Billy and I took off this fag's apartment. While HE/SHE was there too! I had strange moments in my life FOR REAL!

John, who is this woman from England that buys my stuff? She can write me and collect from you. What do you think of that?

If the FEDS magazines put ME in there I'll be Hannibal for sure. "EAT THIS, BABE." HAHA.

David Berkowitz killed only 3!

The best way to be a true Jack the Ripper is to shave all hair off your body. Get naked and go to work on your subject. Cool, don't you agree?

All of Ted Bundy's victims were pretty. He fucked them ALL! I should have made angels of all of MINE! Pull their lungs out their backs and give them wings. If there is a HELL, I'll see Mr. Bundy. We'll share moments. HAHA Bet a lot of cunt would be there...

I agree, sex by itself does NOT satisfy the mind and heart!

When I am able, I'll make up more clover wheels. So far I've only picked one clover of the year.

Martial arts: YES--don't ask: Get a book on pressure points on the body. STUDY it. Then you'll know what I know. Chokeholds I use one hand for. Simple: I can use two fingers, John, and you'd do what I tell you, or go where I go! People ask me to prove it. I ask them to sign a waiver before I do. This way I don't get into any trouble and can't be sued!

Easter was like any other day in here.

Mummify a head in salt--NO: But with VINEGAR, SALT AND LEMON JUICE I MIGHT! First you remove everything inside the body. HEART, LUNGS, STOMACH, INTESTINES AND OTHER ORGANS.

Military hardware is not in a store, but in a

depot--UNDERGROUND! Nuclear warheads--HUNDREDS of them near Syracuse, N.Y.! Different places around this country are depots of storage deep in the ground. Nuclear warheads I'd not go near, but other stuff I would. Picture the U.S.A. going to war with CHINA: They have a HUNDRED MILLION SOLDIERS. We have SHIT--A BIG BLUFF!

Certain parties are begging for my art work. I know you sell stuff for I gave you that permission. But no one else knows this. It keeps things on an even level.

No visit this day. So it looks like Saturday, Sunday and Monday.

Man, I have one heck of a headache. They have been starting again. Won't be long before another seizure hits me. I'll spend another week in the hospital.

I did some wiring this afternoon. Heavy duty shit in the 440 volt range and 30 amps! Big job at a slow pace. And when the switch was thrown I was across the room. Everything worked fine. I was a bit scared though! Speaking of which…thunder showers moving in. I look at the sky and see huge thunderheads.

I'm going fishing in a few minutes on the chow line. FISH + TATERS.

Quite a few guys are getting lockup for not standing at count times--7 AM, 11:55 AM AND 5 PM. I am up at 4 to 4:30 AM each day. Sometimes at 5:30 AM.

I am burning musk oil to purify the air in my room. Somebody is shitting their heart out! Be cool, pal. Gotta run and clean up this apartment.

Later,

Art

The casual revelation by Shawcross of his hitchhiking encounter as a teenager with an apparently homosexual man initially caught me off balance, but it did make a through-the-looking-glass kind of sense. Shawcross seemed to be an omnisexual, in it for the raw pleasure more than an auto-piloted surrender to the gender. Although, he definitely leaned toward women, for better or worse. Usually for worse, as handily evidenced by the cluster-fuck of murders, mutilations, riverside necrophilia, and coffee-break cannibalism.

Cannibalistic tendencies, the modification of the soul by physical internalization of the ultimate "target audience," were other things gnawing and gnashing at me, often-discussed components in the Shawcross Connection. In the end, it was usually the cannibalism that drew me in like an eternally seductive lover leading me into a bedroom where the door to leave never opens again.

CHAPTER SEVEN

Despite the series of traumas and betrayals on both ends of the table, and my overzealous oral fixation, I've still been open to dating. Any relationship seemed like it could be a lot of fun, right up until the attempted murder. All good things come to an end, sooner or later.

The closest I've been to a "meaningful relationship" with a woman as of late were the dismal duo of hookers I smoked crack with one night running the streets of Chelsea. Jesus hung out with hookers too, I figured. Although, Christ probably didn't smoke crack with them. There may be a differential of ideologies. But I have thought that turning pebbles to rocks of crack cocaine would've made for an interesting piece of Biblical apocrypha.

Ember, the part-time prostitute from one of my better temp jobs, was of the few women with whom I shared my Shawcross connection. Maybe, at the time, it was to further impress her or it was my enjoyment of shocking people, or maybe I'd simply drunk too much rum on an empty stomach after our shift was over as she walked home with me to the bunker. Amused, she quickly categorized me as being like the Columbine mass murderers. No one is better at first dates than me.

Any skin-on-skin contact with a woman sitting beside me on the subway train ends up being something I come to cherish as an almost sacred event. Though, at times, I've had to double and triple check to make sure it's a woman.

Sometimes I have to be satisfied with a close enough determination.

Being bizarre does have its drawbacks, occasionally bordering on nursing a multiple personality disorder because of the necessity to socialize (however superficially) in ways which don't terrify people and make them call the police (which usually happens anyway). The intoxicating waters of the abyss run through my veins, though, and so, gives everything I do a hue of critically antichrist sensibilities.

Once in a while, my obsessions presented as situations too close for comfort when it came to everyone involved.

JOHN:

This MANBEEF company is suspect! I need to inspect their layout. I am an EXPERT. HAHA But one never knows these days! I'd also like to know the history of the subject that is to be butchered. One can't ever be too careful in this day and age. An AIDS infected human is no good. But if you had a cool, walk-in type refrigerator with a light you can hang your carcass upside down for a few days to drip out. AIDS dies along with its hosts...Or so I'm informed. Besides--"man beef" does not look like it's shown in the picture. It could be a STING OPERATION BY THE F.B.I. Think about it. MANBEEF calls for killing the subject. In fact, MURDER any way you call it. Think about this John--To become a member you will be asked lots of questions and might BECOME someone's next meal. HAHA BAD TO THE BONE!!!

YES to your question of tastes of different people of the world. ...Smile... BEEN THERE!

Now John, why a white female? Don't you realize that any female skinned looks the same?! You can't tell who is WHAT after that, pal! Believe me, I know firsthand...Just don't order any HOT DOGS. HAHA

I've heard of eBay stopping the sale of serial killer related items. There is a website in Canada that sells anything or so I'm told. I have been working on a new ink art item. Lots of detail. By taking my time I get good results.

That Taylor woman wants me in every way. John-- Some letters are full of perfume scent and an imprint of her pussy. Now THAT I lay on my face HAHA! Taylor Made goes both ways, but prefers females.

I had a nosebleed earlier on one side. That time of the month. I let it drip into a cup. Almost half full before it quit. I could scare the shit out of a guard, pour it all over me and just lay on the floor. HAHA Be my luck and he'd have a HEART ATTACK! Crazy I may be, but fun is fun...

Gotta run, work.

Later,

Art

Early into the twenty-first century, a company popped up on the web called Manbeef, offering what supposedly was human meat for sale. Of course, I couldn't not share the intriguing piece of information with Art. In the end, however, it turned out to be a hoax, unfortunately, but in my drunken and generally mad mental fog I thought I'd discovered a relatively legitimate backdoor to try out cannibalism in a quality and sustained way. Too good to be true, I recall thinking. After Shawcross mentioned that it could be a sting, I came out of my haze long enough to re-consider having entered my personal information on the Manbeef website. It wouldn't be surprising if I were on a watch list with one agency or another somewhere.

Hello John,

How is the ole pal doing of late? On this end I am ok except for minor aches of the old. HAHA

This million dollar bill you sent me is glued to my wall--over my desk inside a plastic sleeve. A BILLION dollar bill--now THAT is going to be the best!

Hey, we first seen HANNIBAL this past week. Pretty gruesome but I could do it much better. I'll have REAL GUTS. HAHA When Hannibal sliced open that cop he should have made it look more real. When guts come out of the body at that height they are still connected inside, not a puddle on the ground. Fried brains looked good though! That sucker ate his own brains. HAHA Cool movie though.

Going to Maine? I am glad. Beautiful state and most of the people are of a better quality than elsewhere! When is the move? Don't overdo it.

Man, I laid down for a few and two hours passed by. Well, I can sit and work on this letter again. Wish I had access to a computer! My Helene the mortician can sleep next to me. But I'd not be sleeping, nor she either. HaHa. She would be WELL worn out first. I'll get an 'A' for that!

People who send out to get photos developed should know that it is controlled by the F.B.I.! They are alerted to suspicious shit.

John, I still get dizzy a bit by laying on my head to the left side a certain way. Weird.

My French lady will be up to visit soon. Hope she

has a skirt on! Let my fingers explore maybe. She is coming on Wednesday--HAHA Me too...

Our girl Maria is heavy! About 180 lbs. I have a photo. A WHOLESOME GIRL she is! But she'd give me a hot time of it! I would like to nibble on that one. HAHA Right--CHEW THE FAT--SHAVE THE PUSSY. No hairballs...

Clara came yesterday. Good day for us both. She will be back in three weeks. It took her 5 hours to drive here. One asshole in the visiting room spoke out loud that "that guy over there (ME) EATS PEOPLE". He's in this unit! I'll have to CONVERSE with him!

I have a request: On future stuff you send off the internet, can you cut off the bottom and top lines? As it is it's not allowed. But some get through. I got a ticket over this. They call it CONTRABAND. But a lot of other stuff was taken too. Like my art supplies once again--NO PERMIT! At the hearing I'll go to this week I'll ask for permits on all my stuff.

On the picture sent, mob-related = do not smash in your face. They SHOOT you! A crushed face means your mouth got the better of you. When you owe money, you get beat up (or a relative). Next time, an arm or leg gets broke. Then you have a choice: EITHER-OR: One in the head behind the ear!

I too want CREMATION.

Maybe I am alien born. Smile

In the near future, I will hit the world news! Wait pal. I've lawyers on the roll...

Two new dinosaurs found in Mexico. Somewhere in remote Mexico are some STRANGE creatures. Seen every now and then. What ARE they and just where do they come from? A question MANY HAVE ASKED!

A trussed up gal is quite tasty. Better a gal than the other!

Vietnamese people taste different than an American. More healthy and leaner. Latina meat--HOT + SPICY. HAHA I made another hot sauce: "Killer Ketchup" Why the hell not? I am what I am. Am I not?!

Got another card from Queens, N.Y. Another blonde. But this one is 64. Who cares at this point?!

My lady in Spain needs pain to get heated up. Bend over, doll, I'll give you pain and then some. HELP HAHA

Time to shut down and get ready for the day ahead. Be good.

Later,

Art

There is a crack in this world somewhere and some very exotic evil is flooding in.

This explains a lot, including, perhaps, Shawcross himself. Me too, as for my own morbid patterns and passions. I do seriously wonder where mental flashes such as vigorous waterfalls of slit-throat blood or having a museum dedicated to the decapitated originate from in the whole world. It is curious wiring. Thankfully, I'm able to redirect most of this into my writing. Most. It could easily have taken a scarier turn and still could if I'm not as mindful as I need to be. Occasionally, every once in a while, as I'm somewhere walking loose, I realize what I'm suddenly thinking matches up to something out of a horror movie, as though I'm in the mind of Jason Voorhees, for example. It comes back to me that I once invited Freddy Krueger to my thirteenth birthday party (the actor who played Krueger, Robert Englund did reply with a gracious hand-written letter apologizing that he couldn't make it and was occupied with the Nightmare on Elm Street TV series Freddy's Nightmares). I just try to make sense of it.

My appearance is quite conventional and as elegant as budget permits. No one would have an obvious reason to believe that I am any sort of threat. Then I remember that my psychiatrist felt the community should be protected from me. I attempt to lighten the tension by injecting some humor; imagining a Charlie Chaplin scenario with me chasing a decapitated head down the street as I haplessly kick it just out of reach like the slapstick star would chase feverishly after his bowler hat having somehow fallen off. I don't tell my psychiatrist about this. Not many mental health professionals I've ever met have shared my sense of humor.

There are certainly gray areas to examine, at least philosophically.

The idea of cannibalism and eccentric concepts like collecting heads is a form of worship, not necessarily destruction, or hateful decimation. To my mind, anyway. The sacramental preservation of sentimental creations. It's the adoring separation of those held in only the highest regard from the madness of a malfunctioning world, and providing a safe haven and the rarefied calm of the black temple--an invisible Eden with roots extending into the very cellular makeup of the cannibal. The heads, for the altar; the body, for the soul and symbiotic union.

And then, there was the Shawcross cut of cannibalism, who took a more ungodly tact with his...eating habits. Whatever bits and pieces he decided to consume were not for communion but, basically, in the category of snacks rather than something sacred. This is where he and I differed on our views. But it was the same with the subject of women as a general matter. I see ladies as worshipful and divinely majestic spirits. Shawcross was quite brutally blunt with his own misogyny and objectification. He did, however, see himself as a "mutant", while I primarily prefer to think of myself as a misunderstood and unconventional priest of sorts. So, we certainly weren't on the same page with some key matters. We were just two disjointed people whose lives happened to have intersected and somehow meshed. No relationship is perfect, though. For sure, we had our good days and our bad.

Excerpt from Mental Health Evaluation for "Mr. John Fay"

According to an East Boston police report dated 2/29/12, upon arrival, a male party reported that Mr. Fay cut him in the throat with a knife and was bleeding from the neck. Mr. Fay allowed police to search the apartment but a knife could not be located. Shortly thereafter, the defendant was pat frisked and a knife was located in his jacket pocket. Upon interview about the incident, Mr. Fay stated that his friend began committing a lot of crimes and it made the defendant uncomfortable. He remarked, "He liked to go around robbing people... (It was) almost a bragging thing... I knew better than to involve myself." On that particular day, "He tried to assault me, he didn't want to leave (my apartment)... I had possession of a knife... I don't know what happened in the chaos...The case was dismissed, he never showed up to court."

My relationships, for one reason or another, were dramatically narrowing. Even as the connection with Shawcross started to fracture I often re-read his correspondence to lift the weight of isolation.

Mental Health Evaluation excerpt:

When (court clinician) initially inquired about his charge of Threatening to Commit a Crime involving (ex-girlfriend Alyssa), Mr. Fay discussed his perception that events were "blown out of proportion" and commented that, "I haven't had many relationships in my life."

As a retrospective note to self and all interested parties, I truly doubt the above excuses or even abstractly explains, alleged strangulation, purported projections of removal of said girlfriend's head, and possibly attempted murder, but such is life in Fay World. Which brings us to the following, very apropos segue of Shawcross' supposed Biblical concurring on love...which he claimed to write, but is in reality from 1 Corinthians 13:4-7.

LOVE

BY ARTHUR JOHN SHAWCROSS

05/21/98

LET ME TELL YOU OF LOVE:

LOVE IS PATIENT AND LONG ENDURING:

IT IS KIND, NEVER ENVYING,

NEVER AMBITIOUS FOR ITSELF,

NEVER PUTTING ON AIRS,

OR DISPLAYING ITSELF HAUGHTILY:

IT BOASTS NOT.

LOVE IS NEVER VAIN, NEVER ARROGANT,

NEVER PUFFED UP WITH PRIDE,

LOVE BEHAVES IN A SEEMLY MANNER,

NEVER RUDE OR UNBECOMING.

LOVE SEEKS NOT ITS OWN REWARD,

NOR MAKES DEMANDS,

BUT GIVES ITSELF WITH ALL.

LOVE DOES NOT PERSEVERE TO ITS OWN BENEFIT:

IT IS NOT FRETFUL, OR RESENTFUL.

IT TAKES NO ACCOUNT OF EVIL DONE TO IT.

AND PAYS NO HEED TO WRONG IT SUFFERS.

YET, IT DOES NOT REJOICE AT INJUSTICE.

BUT LOVE WILL NEVER END.

"AND SO, THREE THINGS ABIDE FOREVER:

FAITH, HOPE, AND LOVE.

AND THE GREATEST OF THESE IS LOVE."
Even love, however, has its limits.

Hi John,

No Sir, ALL is NOT WELL! Still no word out of my wife!

Let's not bother Maria. I'd take her for a stroll along a lonely path and talk about whatever we may want.

Well pal, I've gotten my first HATE MAIL. One of the victim's nieces. Maybe I can fuck her mind over. She wanted to STRANGLE me, take my eyes out, cut off my dick, make me bleed to death slowly. My-my, such language from a woman! Her aunt was a WHORE-- but a "good mother". RIGHT, SURE THING! John, I can tease this cunt by saying I know what we talked about when she died and it wasn't about no little wannabe whore like you! But instead I turned that letter into the Administration. This way I am covered from bullshit down the road. Really that letter is threatening.

MY TURN...LOVE IT!

YOU my loyal pal, thanks for the birthday wish to my wife.

How is your cousin doing with her pregnancy? Most likely ready to lose instant weight. Hey John, ever have breast milk? It's sticky--just like cunt juice. Cunt juice works wonders as a face cream. TRY it. Wish I had some: My face is chopped on place. I just peeled another patch of dead skin! AGENT ORANGE! Now you flood the face of a female with sperm and rub it in. Be sure to kiss her BEFORE you do so. HAHA

Well now. We have a black female in here. Has a face a dog would bark at. Fuck it--I'd roll her over and drive one in her. But after I poured a shot of whiskey into her cunt. If she screams, DON'T fuck it! Any fool will do the both of us as long as she is--or isn't-- willing.

That WD-40 really is something else. Spray it on and rub it in good. Works for ME! Hey man I am ALREADY CRAZY--Side effects would make me NORMAL. HAHA

GOODDAMN THESE 3 LIVE COUNTS A DAY! Morning, noon, and evening. Before, only bodies were counted. You get written up if found DEAD.

HAHA!

Almost half the year gone and still NO VISIT. Time to invite women to come in ANYTIME. If my WIFE shows up, send her in--Join the get-together.

John, I married Clara July 10, 1997. 4 YEARS AGO. I have not laid her yet. I feel deep in my bones that SOMEONE GOT IN BEFORE ME!!! Can't wear it out: Pliable like rubber.

SHIT, at 70 it IS rubber. HAHA

Hunting deer was a challenge for real! I'd go out every Friday night in the fall and winter with a .22 or a 410 shotgun. One or two a week. No drippings in my driveway like your Native American friend's father with his deer. Once you've shot your first deer with no ill effects it becomes BETTER. Just like hunting HUMANS...

Man, I came in soaking wet! Another day using a power sprayer on the floor.

I am working on another Spiderman. I've three so far. The new Spiderman movie is coming out soon. I've got one drawing for you. Soon as I get it set up I'll ship it. Last evening I drew up a T-Rex. Got to give it more teeth. Now I should put a gal in its mouth to make your day John. HAHA I just might...

I did a small vinyl for my wife last night also. Stayed up past 10 pm and got up at about 7:45 AM.

Well, my hearing aid did not come in. I wanted the left side and was given the RIGHT. I would bet these things work good in the woods while hunting. But be sure to turn them off before SHOOTING. HAHA OUCH!

I went to see our doctor today and he told me he is giving me special medication for my feet. Take once a day for 90 days. I said OK. Then a nurse calls me later to tell me I have to be seen taking a pill each day. I refused and also refused to sign a refusal slip! I'm not a fucking baby, nor am I a RETARD! In August when I see the doctor again I'll inform him at that time to LEAVE ME ALONE--DON'T CALL ME. I'll refuse to show up. Doctors say one thing, nurses another.

I'll put this in an envelope and seal it up. Got some work to do. Write when you are able.

Later,

Art

The awakening sometime during the night when I was fifteen--a crucial, fast-track year for my dark-sider evolution--would place me in a category into which I couldn't have intentionally positioned myself. Nor would I have cared to. And it was way too freaky to initiate or entertain a discourse over in most courteous, civilized get-togethers, such an ominous situation of impending domestic cannibalism. Like so many other things whirling and winding through the dank corridors of my mind, I hadn't any relevant idea of the source of the spontaneous, starving desperation to procure a Whitman's Sampler of human flesh. It was real, though, and... so powerful. It pulsed and swirled with a seemingly supernatural wrath as a trippy, netherworld sensation of falling in love coupled with an orgasmic infusion of lust for the shining pinnacle of forbidden consummation. Complete consumption.

Perhaps disturbingly, it was as though I was familiar already with the practice, something natural. A tingling warm-bath feeling moving like an exhilarating melody on my skin and into my muscles, zipping through my veins in a manner that I later would compare to the mellifluous, everything-is-ok feeling of heroin. The alchemical transmuting of lead to light; a brief apotheosis--the epic elevation from the mortal boxes and a relieving flashbulb-fast liberation from bearing my own burdensome body.

The element of possession by some malevolent spirit again comes into question. Although this may explain it, it wouldn't excuse it. It simply feels at times like a conglomeration of wilding gremlins crammed past capacity into my skull and a sapping Beast force keeping me tethered to a Hell sleigh. It's a road leading to cramped, windowless rooms in the heart of high-crime areas, police station holding cells, county jails, lockdown hospital wards, drunken misadventures into cemeteries (using a grave marker as a makeshift pillow), and even the obscurity of living--and almost dying--in the deep woods (the same woods where I found the perfect tree to hang myself). Does anyone know how hard it is to get your mail in the woods? Very few in modern society will have the firsthand understanding of getting your letters delivered to "The Woods". And, as paranoia begins to saturate all sense of reason (which it, sooner or later, will) you'll eventually suspect the squirrels of stealing your mail. You'll see them watching you, following you in a perfectly synchronized stalking routine, and start to believe that they're planning on having you killed. They'd do it themselves, you'll somehow understand, but squirrels are usually too squeamish for murder. It's a conundrum all right. You may end up in a mental institution over it. But at least you'll get your mail there--when the other patients aren't busy eating it.

Now, like the drinking which breaches doorways, and being aware of it beforehand, I am consciously deciding to indulge and invoke the demon. Curiosity, in this case, may have led to monstrosity, blindly engaging in random occult sciences and black arts.

Hi John,

My uncle is buried at the bottom of a mountain in cement with his motorcycle. You won't hear of any African artifacts found there. UFOs maybe! Picture that, you say New Hampshire a part of Africa! Not likely. But you never know.

John, I did not mean I'd shoot just ANY women or men, but DRUG DEALERS! The first woman had a packet of tiny blue + black envelopes--COCAINE.

I do have to make a new batch of Killer Ketchup. I'll try to get another tiny Zip Lock and send it.

Taylor's last real name begins with an A. That much I've found out.

I've tied up at least one. Left wrist to right ankle--right wrist to left ankle. SPREAD LIKE A CHRISTMAS GOOSE. Makes for an interesting meal. But of course DUCT TAPE over mouth. She was the sleeper...

A spaceship full of women, all will be fucked by me at least once. Keep the good ones, the SPECIALS. Save a few not so good ones for sport. COOK some. Even send them outside for a quick reminder to the ones who don't cooperate fully! Make them watch the results! HAHA COOL MAN.

Thanks for the address labels. Where can those $200 bills be ordered? My boss wants to know. One officer took the last bill you sent and now I find CAN have it--But the officer gave it to his wife. So he says. Oh, he also says he's sorry! BULLSHiT!

I worked myself to dead tiredness on Friday cutting glue from an old tile concrete floor. Lift the tiles and you've got a BITCH of a job! Monday I'll be out in the halls driving the power scrubber. I am going to sleep now pal.

Later,

Art

Note: Shawcross included for me a dessert recipe, which I assume might follow well a tasty meal of thigh on rye and palm salad!

PEANUT BUTTER PING PONG BALLS

1 tsp vanilla

½ cup honey

½ cup peanut butter

2-3 Rice Krispies cereal

Mix vanilla, honey, and peanut butter together in a large bowl. Stir in Rice Krispies cereal until all mixed together. Wet hands and shake off excess water. Start forming ping pong size "balls" out of your mix and set on wax paper or tin foil.

It will be necessary to wet your hands several times during this process.

When finished, set them in the refrigerator. Best served chilled!

By Arthur J. Shawcross

2001

Regarding the perennial "mystery" of the undercover super-deviant, I've mostly solved what remains shrouded and secreted. It's a menacing energy that can eat anyone alive. If it becomes aware that it's seen--spotlighted in the shadowy, recessed gutter where it's been squirming, slithering, and shamelessly pulsating--it quickly graduates into a lethal perception of the exoteric world which, logically, you know has to be kept in check. The key is to acknowledge and appreciate it for the power, courage, and unimpeded direction it allows you.

You have to shed your humanity and become steel; a directed reptilian force free from the agonizing softness of the human experience. It's clarity with no emotional diversions. A spontaneous injection of euphoria elicited by a thought: that you probably are the most dangerous person wherever you are. No foreign substances necessary. The perception of this power can propel some people into madness. A pure, virgin energy and consumptive wrath which either warps or shields and empowers. One can't, however, be wholly both human and (for the sake of simplicity) demon. The two are far too extreme to exist together and will potentially destroy the host. It's best, one realizes, to excise any connections to that which makes one weak and emotionally disembowels; this conspiratorial disease of excessive emotion.

The genius of the demon is effective manipulation and entrancing projection of its host's persona.

Walking among them, quietly traversing an invisible sub-region. By comparison, the average people are dancing in a metaphorical penthouse and the afflicted, but ironically empowered, drags monsters through the streets chained to his ankles, existing within the very fabric of nightmares. Although, of course, it does have its intensely intoxicating and rewarding moments. And an UPDATE from the sewers of Hell brought to you by Arthur Shawcross:

John, that Man Beef advertisement was looked into by my boss on his computer. Said he was asked many questions pertaining to his health, asked for his phone number and address at his HOUSE, NOT A

P.O. BOX! Bet they were setting him up to be the next item up for sale! HAHA GOOD MOVE...

Human meat has a flavor somewhat like a pot roast when well done. BEEN there pal, did that! But mine was roasted over an open fire. Quite good actually.

* * *

Hi John,

Man, it's been a hard way to go in this country of late. Now the news is stating that there were more planes to crash on that day--9/11/01.

I am quite angry over this that I am not in a position for fighting the RAGHEADS or whomever is responsible!

I have seen "THE SILENCE OF THE LAMBS" movie.

And about the Donner Party, it is said that those people only had five miles to walk. But if you recall, it was snowing quite hard and they did not know direction. I WOULD have survived. Don't YOU think?!

In today's world it is better to cook your meat through. Smile

What type of place are you going for in Maine? Backwoods type or secluded shoreline?

Wish I had a BILLION DOLLARS to play with-the REAL, pal, THE REAL!

John, as soon as I'm given another blood test, then

I'll be going into a hospital to get my blood thinned out. It is too thick and can KILL ME! I am at 54% hemoglobin. Normal is 42%! A needle in one arm going to a machine another needle in the other arm to return the thinned out blood. Hope I'm asleep when it's going on or I'll pass out anyway! Am In anxious? YES...Maybe my hair will grow back. HAHA I am really going thin on top!

Got another blonde gal pal. She is 26, 5'11" tall and married--AN OPEN MARRIAGE! She (MELISSA) lives in Carlisle, Pennsylvania. Claims to come and visit. Wants to touch me! Wonder where...HAHA This I'll check out even if her husband shows up.

Have not heard from Maria in a while. Wonder if she passed on to other people to connect with! I like that woman for some reason I can't describe truthfully. Must be magnetism of sorts. She'd sure keep me warm in the winter.

I am getting sleepy. Catch you later.

Art

P.S. How is Boston doing with the situation on the Towers?

As the Towers came down, right as they were becoming dust, so too was my faltering life.

I hadn't realized until around noon September 11th that the world was coming to an end. I oozed off the futon in the parlor of the bunker, which was generally lit only by a floor-to-ceiling color-changing water lamp, after another late night spent generously doused in rum. Hazily I was aware, in a hung over dream-like sense, of explosions replaying on the big screen TV. For no immediately explicable reason, all twelve of my shrunken heads were set up on the floor. With wobbly legs, I stepped cautiously so as to not kick over or damage any of them. I was in a disgusting state: oblivious, in my underwear (uncertain of where my eyeglasses or pants were, which was also becoming very normal), and, just in case I wilted to the nausea, looking for the least undignified place to vomit, which would probably end up being the floor since I couldn't spot the barrel without eyeglasses-- and I couldn't find my eyeglasses without my eyeglasses. But that was just me settling in to my damnation. Just an average morning really. Suddenly, though, I had snippets of flashbacks, of me lecturing the heads the night before on nothing even approaching reasonable subject matter. Normal things.

Hi John,

Lately I have been OK health wise. Just stressed out to the MAX.

Looks like my Christmas will be Shitsville! Not one fucking word from the woman I married! I guess the HYPE wore off and she's out FUCKING WHOMEVER WILL TAKE HER! Not a good thing to say of one's wife, but it's true just the same. Looks like another divorce in the making.

That bullshit with the FEDS. magazine is enough for me to kill those fuckers! Try as you might, they NEVER get the story straight. That I will sue them for, plus I didn't sign any release form for them to print ANYTHING! I have that article out of the magazine--PHOTOCOPIED NO LESS! If they EVER come back, I will do damage to one of them at least!!!

My WTC sketch and painting went to NYC.

Did you know some trees are blossoming! Even tulips and daffodils are blooming. Some cherry trees have blossoms.

BOOKS OF BLOOD. Yah, I need a drink of some REAL stuff!

GOOD on Global Warming--Melt the ice caps, flood the coastlines back 500 miles. Might clean up some slums, don't you think?!

I've seen tornadoes up close out in Oklahoma, 1968. I watched one flip trailers and suck up all the water, mud and fish, from a pond! Those catfish had to be 20 LBS or MORE! Where did they go? When I was a kid I'd jump into a dust devil twister of grass and twigs. Some knocked me over!

OSAMA BIN LADEN'S HEAD SHRUNKEN??? FUCK, SHRINK HIS WHOLE BODY WITH HIS OWN DICK IN HIS MOUTH AND A LOUISVILLE SLUGGER BASEBALL BAT UP HIS ASS! But...he is only ONE ASSHOLE of MANY involved.

We got hit with snow 2 and half inches on the ground--More on the way. Soon you may see some coming your way, or this was an accident.

John, I am wound up tight over my wife. If I don't get answers soon, then this old boy is going to be locked up again for REAL this time!

Later,

Art

CHAPTER EIGHT

My father has referred to me as a "killer". It isn't true of course. One actually has to kill someone to live up to such a distinction. And yet, he is the one who counseled me, in his wicked wisdom, on how to hurt, terrorize, manipulate, and mind control people and groups. What he didn't seem to understand, ultimately, was that he couldn't teach someone to be at least as brutal as he was and still have a convenient victim handily available in me. It could and would only go one way or another. The man created his own doom.

My father already had a natural born instinct in the darker areas of human control and hunting, but he also intently studied the assassins, intelligence, and counter-intelligence, and aspired to work as a government assassin himself. Despite his insanity, he was quite a scholarly mind. As a matter of fact, Dad was associated with Naval intelligence and chosen to work for the FBI soon after I was thrust into his life. He made the decision to forego the FBI gig because, as Dad has said with obvious chagrin, he hadn't wanted to move the family to Washington, D.C. where the job was based. My opinion is that he resented us all for having had to make such a life re-defining choice. Oh, well...I didn't get my mother pregnant with myself--or I'd be writing a very different book and making a fortune on the talk show and circus circuit. Another missed opportunity, I lament. So, evidently, Poppa settled for the subtle agony of mediocrity. Although, not exactly comfortably. Hence, his drinking problem. Projecting his feelings about the choices he felt he was forced to make, he's told me numerous times never to get married. Sometimes, in his drunken rants, warning me, "I'll blow your head off if you ever get married."

Needless to say (but I'll say it anyway), I've always had reservations about marriage and, my overall views on relationships have been distorted badly. Unfortunately, it seems to be irreversible. It couldn't be avoided really. He planted toxic seeds in my formative years and it's just something that I need to work through to the best of my disability, and it's not getting any better as time goes on. I can see the sunshine, but it's shining on someone else's face. I've had such off-putting and odd dynamics with females. Maddeningly, what initially seemed lovely alignments have been hate-breeding incubators of MIS-alignments, either platonic or atomic. And in the end, I always find myself slithering back into the shadow of my own approaching extinction, rolling in like the clouds of some final storm.

Perhaps it bears a dishonorable mention that I watched him when I was about five years old strangle my mother nearly to death. And then, while they were separated for a year from the ages of ten to eleven, he would take me with him to stalk my mother. There's an engraved image in my mind that I'll never be able to wipe away of Dad playing his favorite Led Zeppelin on his 1985 Camaro stereo and drinking a bizarrely oversized beer as we circled my grandmother's house where my mother was staying during the trial separation and restraining order period. Ironically--with the typical overtones of oddity and undertones of Freudian trips of unspecified perversity--it was the best year of my childhood with those people. My initiation and well-earned first degrees of dealing with and managing mutants. I developed into something ghastly in my own right, but they were grotesque, and missed the mark on meeting the criteria for human beings by light years. There is dark but then there is evil. They and Shawcross were straight from the depths of some obscure, out of the way lake in an undisclosed location in Hell. Pure badness.

This is what I romance: love and death; sunsets and funerals; and inaccessible women in positions of authority. I am a passionate romantic with a heart of fire and wrath, while my parents and controversially chosen surrogate father figure, Arthur Shawcross, were missing their hearts. Though--lemon to lemonade, water to wine…ashes to ashes--at least, Shawcross was (in his way) interesting and (in his way) interested in what was going on with me. Something from Tales from the Crypt, perhaps, but it's who I am, and there is a clear paucity in my ability to bond with anyone who is NOT a criminal, creep, call girl, or cannibal. So be it.

Hi JOHN,

Thanksgiving was a bomb. Piss poor BULLSHIT given to us! I would have had more enjoyment eating out a FEMALE GUARD! 2 ounces of processed turkey we got! Right in the garbage it went. The STARVING assholes ate it though!

I've three sketches of the Trade Center. The plane that crashed on Veterans Day was an accident. Engine fell off and stabilizer broke. This section came off! Weird though.

Teeth problems, eh? Shit--join the crowd of NO TEETH at all. HAHA

I've had two light bulbs go out the same day.

Did you know that a crater of Pluto was ten miles deep and 4 wide?! You could hide a ship in there…

You and I WON'T BE ALIVE when that rock comes our way out of deep space. No place to hide if we WERE! Underground cities, yes, but no natural light--might as well be in a subterranean PRISON! Let them have their tunnels and cities.

Let's DIE LIKE MEN up here! Fuck as many as you can and then evaporate just you CUM!

Speaking of cumming... Your cousin had a baby girl--ok! Looks like momma, daddy, or the MILKMAN... or ME. HAHA

America needs a lift up badly! But then again it needs to be spanked as well. Leave other countries alone! America wants to dominate the world...

Be good.

Later,

Art

P.S. Get a copy of the FEDS magazine. I am in there!

Occasionally, I was ambivalent about having mentioned my pregnant cousin to Shawcross. Only during brief moments of sobriety, of course, in general. It was concerning that Shawcross might perceive or misinterpret certain perversions in me. Then I reminded myself who I was talking to--and also, recall the same cousin (as well as her older sister and even my contemporary male cousin) flashing me every intimate part of herself while we were all growing up. Things like that stick with you. Sharing such secrets sometimes felt necessary for me, to alleviate or mitigate the tension of suppressing some very potent and potentially acutely damaging memories. But, as had become almost protocol, there was no one I could share my mind-boggling past with except one of America's most demented cannibals. Positioned as I was somewhere in the hinterlands between Wonderland and Oz, it was the more sensible thing to do.

Being the surrogate parent he was to me, he was the kind of parental figure who is also a best friend and confidant.

When the Jehovah's Witnesses first came to the dollhouse sometime during the late 1990s, I was the one who answered the door. Bless their hearts. They were a young man and a compatibly-aged blonde woman. The name I got from the girl was Jacqueline, who I found to be to my taste. The male's name wasn't particularly important to me. Deciding to humor them then, I accepted their invitation to the local Kingdom Hall. I agreed to meet them that night. The main attraction was of course Jacqueline, spontaneously envisioning her as the centerpiece of a Kingdom Hall super-orgy. But as usual in my misadventures with women, it was a substantial disappointment. Not only was there not even the most rudimentary of orgies when I arrived but I barely got to say a word to Jacqueline when I saw her at the talk. Except that I did manage to invite them back to the dollhouse for the next afternoon with the promise of listening to more of their pitch for recruitment.

Hi John,

Thanks for the card, man. Cool DEAD SHOT you sent. Looks good enough to EAT. Nice TITS. Why is she hung up?

"AH!" Now we understand the reason of the cut open one. Was she HIGH? HAHA! It's a good thing I didn't find that girl hanging! I'd have done feet up and SKINNED OUT -- BLED OUT TOO! Nigger chop -- BLACK BACON...SPARE RIBS. She has to cool 72 hours hung up skinned.

This shrunken head picture is cool in itself. Now THERE is a job for ME... SHRUNKEN HEADS, EH?! Swamp man in Florida selling them? Your heads resemble Jamaicans. HAHA...OK by ME.

I'D not touch their women! They fuck and DON'T CLEAN UP. Funky for real, Man!

It's 2:59 AM and the Moon is full with a star on its upper right side. Clear and cool outside. Hey, crocks and gators love niggers. Feed them the Jamaicans.

Yup, a corned farm girl. One that has NOT been fucked by a horse! Picture a herd of naked females out behind the barn eating grass and oats naked, down on all fours. Do we MILK them? You bet! Feed them no meat, all veggies. You'll have to hose them down now and then to get the crud off!

SHAVED PUSSY I LIKE -- but only the PUSSY LIPS. Hair can be shaved and shaped into many things. I've sucked a lot of pussy in my day. Young, teenage, middle years, mature and old. Older is firmer. Young is tasty.

Jehovah's Witnesses people are so cool...and stupid -- a wee bit GULLIBLE too!!! I had them in my place and we debated all day. Two women. We had tea. Or, they had tea and I had thee after a while. Gave both a MICKEY. MY PLAYTHINGS. Had to hide their car. Still there I bet. Rusted out for real! Oh, those people have a good argument, but it's all their way or NO way. They thought they were so pure but WEREN'T VIRGINS. Back when I was 22 I had one and ALL OF TWO. Washington Park they do abide FOREVER! I wonder if they were missed?! Depoleville, New York was their stomping grounds. A small, deep valley. Hill going in and out.

Zecharia Sitchin? Not recalled -- can you get a book of his for me? I love reading things of that nature. Thanks.

The END of this world will not come about in our lifetime!

I am a survivor for real.

Joel Norris died of AIDS in California. In fact, he had AIDS when he interviewed me. MAN -- what a lawsuit THAT would have been if I had known at the time!

Norris was a pitcher AND a catcher in L.A. California. Wrote a few books. He is sucking hot cock in HELL now!

John, I have visited Boston. Lived there six months. Your best bet is to live near your parents while they are still with you. Then the Southwest for sure. Warm, dry climate. Stop by HERE -- we can visit for a time.

Big tit women with BABIES GROWING OUT OF THEM. Now THAT sketch I'd like to see!

Last evening while I was out in the recreation area drawing a new sketch, guys asked if I could do family shots. I told them all no. I have in the past -- but you learn the hard way. DON'T FUCK WITH INMATES!

Have a good week, John. Merry Christmas, pal.

Later,

Art

Coincidentally, I bought a razor sharp replica Ninjato sword at a little knife shop on a trip to Boston shortly before I crossed paths with the Jehovah's Witnesses. That katana, I swear, must have been sharpened by some demon in one of its more murderous moods. Playing with the new toy, I enjoyed tossing oranges up in the air and slicing them in half mid-air. Although this was an amusing party trick for a while, I almost cut my sister in half during one of my less coordinated demonstrations. It's what happens when I forego my eyeglasses for the sake of vanity and misplaced pride. Thankfully, no one was hurt, then. Ideas, however, combusted inside of the cool, dimmed privacy of my psychic silver screen shortly after meeting Jacqueline and her goofy, decidedly nameless, male counterpart.

There was obviously no way either of them could've known, or even suspect, that by the time of our next sit-down on the front porch of the dollhouse, I'd already begun to daydream of cutting Jacqueline's head off. It just isn't the kind of thing people tend to worry about. As a guest of mine, decapitating her with a ninja sword wouldn't have been an especially hospitable choice. I do realize these things. Also, I like to think of myself as a gracious host. And surely, there are yet further Freudian undertones within such gruesomely designed blueprints. Although, any connection to conventional sex was, as far as I was consciously concerned, the furthest thing from me. Ms. Jacqueline Jehovah just so happened to have a pretty head on her shoulders. My interest was mainly her artistic value. But I contemplated about how much leeway on creative license the law would have tolerated in this matter?

So, not wanting to take a chance with a Judge Dredd sometime in the future, I made a pact with myself to not take the sword to the upcoming meeting with the Jehovah's Witnesses. Besides, I was still living with my family and they never got me to begin with. They damn well wouldn't understand this: the frosty heads of a blue-eyed Jehovah's Witness and her tag along neatly stored in the family's community freezer. Sweet Satan, where would my dear sister's son put his precious fucking freezer pops? ("MAMA, UNCLE JOHNNY WON'T TAKE HIS HEADS OUT OF THE FREEZER!") Family members are infinitely less accommodating when body parts of random visitors begin showing up around an already cluttered house. And, oh, gee whiz, are BOTH sisters pregnant again? Looks like Johnny has to move his Jehovah's Witnesses down to the basement… with all the other little dead things we buried.

Aside from that, I imagined beheading anyone with the sudden and ferocious swipe of a sword clean through someone's neck--cutting through tendons, carotid arteries, windpipe, and other fleshy and vascular places--would most definitely cause a gushing mega-tsunami and stormy precipitation of BLOOD. Personally, of course, I wouldn't have sweated such a radically unorthodox offering except that the cleanup would be a daunting ordeal. Again, it's the problem of sharing a home with those not willing to let you live your dreams in peace. Another thing is, what if the person didn't quite shut down right away? Would she react like the proverbial chicken, with me stumbling after the headless cadaver-to-be, fountain-bleeding five feet into the air; in my own panic, offering the head back to her as she ran blindly around the house tripping over my mother's godforsaken wicker furniture and our aimlessly meandering cats?

It's always something, or always nothing.

As for the Jehovah's young man, you know what they say about witnesses.

Hey John,

This first photo is a bit on the cut-up side. Now THERE was a man in need of a true disposal unit that could handle a large load. HAHA Like a SAUSAGE MACHINE. I see ole Dahmer was into DARK MEAT!

You ever see MY victim photos on the Web? Hey -- Page 5 is cool in the photo. A broom shoved up her CUNT, OUCH! No splinter there, John. From the side of the broom she's got. 3 feet up inside! Right up next to the heart and throat. Was it self-induced?

Some dildo...

John, at this moment, any woman with a cunt I'd not kick out of bed! Marilyn Monroe gave a lot of head from I read!

Girls are girls -- some easy -- some hard -- some even catch rain up the nose, so to say. STUCK UP! Ever fuck a drunken broad? ANY hole will do...

The biggest thrill to Jehovah's Witnesses is to agree with them until you toss them out. Jehovah's Witnesses...The good part is to butter them up -- suck up to everything they speak on -- Then fuck them for real!

A dumb country gal from West Virginia would put up one hell of a fuck. SUCK IT DOLL. HAHA Do you have a photo of cousin Michelle? Smile. I can dream too.

"Fuck a pregnant woman and you poke a dent in the kid's forehead..."

There are more planets in the solar system than we think! Look at all the galaxies that are being discovered out there! I am getting the Sky & Telescope magazine now. I've two issues so far. This Earth is set for a polar shift on a mass scale. Think of this planet forming land masses. The Pacific is ever changing. A shift is due. But one comes up in one area goes down in another. Many places throughout history were above water but now are not!!!!

The average inmate is an ASSHOLE. As I am not normal that counts me out. HAHA When you bust your skills to draw someone's family and they want the picture before payment -- you get bad vibes on it.

So I don't do for fellow brother and sometimes sister inmates. HAHA

Take Amtrak in Spring & Summer of Northern USA. Stay out of the Midwest and South -- too many derailments!

Joel Norris was a fag for REAL. I tried to sue him but the fucker died before I could get him served with papers!

Send books direct to me -- I pick them up at the package room. I am allowed 24 books a month.

Happy NEW YEAR, Brother.

Arthur

We understood at an almost bleakly comical level the naiveté inherent in anyone--Jehovah's Witnesses, hitchhikers, and hookers especially--talking to strangers. Never mind going out of one's way to visit the stranger in the comfort of his control zone. Some of us out here just aren't normal…

Even my mother warned me never to talk to strangers, and she didn't care about anyone, least of all her own children. A point for appropriate perspective: She was a high school Spanish teacher for an all-girls Catholic school and to this day I barely understand a word of the language, which would've been useful for me in the predominantly Spanish-speaking East Boston.

The jungle, incidentally, isn't the only place where missionaries get eaten by the natives.

Hi John,

How do you cure those Jehovah's Witnesses women? By fucking them! Fuck one, then fuck another--but have that one suck the first one's pussy while you cornhole her. They might like it. HAHA

Some people get brainwashed into thinking they have to go door to door. I knew of a place in in Northern New York called Depoleville that had its own little community of Witnesses. I was fishing in its creek. The girls are so prim and proper until you remove their clothes and kiss the pussy. Then they are yours! Put their clothes back on and they change again! I hate to think what might happen if caught (...)

CHAPTER NINE

Why, exactly, I continued sharing death scene photos with Shawcross must've been some inkling of sinister consideration between friends on the surface of it. To outsiders, perhaps evil. But, from my point of view, I feel that it's more a morbidly obtuse sense of humor, while, also, innately understanding the unique audience I had with Shawcross. It's always been important for me to keep the audience entertained, sparing them the boredom that they already have easy enough access to. Though, I would never deny the trace amounts of malevolence in me; that I do see waves of cascading blood prodigiously flowing from the faces of a passing person or a great torrent of blood speeding to shore out of the Boston Harbor. It seems everyone except for me is involved in happy-ending fuck-fests all around- -and, Hell's bells, where did they find all of those smiles? At times, in my greatest despair, lying in bed alone again, I wonder where the nearest ax store might be. Love may be blind, but blood is a vision.

As for truly crystalline devil's heritage, though, Shawcross was wholeheartedly an O.G. (Original Ghoul). By now, I have no doubt of that extreme classification. Nor had he, making it clear over the years, both in our private dealings and with the media, that he was evil. A "mutant," according to himself.

And sometimes, our paths intertwined with other human monstrosities. Such was the case in our mutual association with the "Vampire of Paris" Nico Claux. Claux was a murderer of some notoriety. Although he had only killed one person, apparently, he did eat some of him, so he had that going for him. After his arrest, a police search of his apartment turned up unidentified skeletal remains that he apparently stole from his job in a morgue, blood bags stolen from a hospital's blood bank, jars filled with human ashes, and hundreds of hardcore S&M videotapes. He was now out of prison and was an artist of some renown; much of his work was portraits of serial killers.

Shawcross and Claux had been in touch for some time, their artwork normally the topic of discussion between them. The same with Claux and me. It was an on-and-off correspondence that started while the vampire was still in prison and then continued for a brief period after his release. I bought numerous portraits from Claux for my own home and to re-sell. The work I bought from him included two or three portraits of Arthur Shawcross (several different Dahmer mug shots too). To the outsider, it may appear that insane life and death styles breed frightening family ties. But madness is the currency of demons, and one just works with what he has.

HEY JOHN,

All is cool on the home front. But in here and outside, MAN it's damn HOT! NO RAIN IN OVER A MONTH!

My leg made it back, only the kneecap is sore yet.

Want to laugh John?! Nico Claux asked me if he could buy my art supplies I need. Well Now--Amends come back to me. I said YES. But the kicker--I send painting or paintings. It's ok; if I get what I ask for. I will cost about $20 to $25 to ship to Sweden! That is where he lives now.

Give me a female that has a tattoo of THIS PUSSY

BELONGS TO SHAWCROSS. HAHA What a TRIP that would be!

Human skin CANNOT make a coat! TOO DAMN THIN!

Some girls after a rape LOVE it and wish it would happen AGAIN--They re-live it in their minds.

Are you "crazy"--WHO IS TO SAY? Am I? HAHA

Take that video of the first plane going into the tower--Slow it right down to slow motion. Then back it up. WILD!

Let's see what else I can send you. Well now, I did not keep a file on what poems I've sent you or whatever. Crazy like a fox. Got one titled "STUPIDITY".

Some nigger has his radio playing black protest of whites, so I blast him with my own shit. Mine says, SHUT THE FUCK UP AND STAND AGAINST THE WALL, ASSHOLE! HAHA

Now that radio is really cranked up. I wish I had a good tape player and certain tapes--make for good sport. HAHA

Guess what John: That MANBEEF company moved to Africa. Closed its doors in this country and split. It seems the FBI got onto them. Lots of DARK MEAT in Africa!

I once read about one village starving and one man was healthy as can be. Others took notice and asked how can he stay healthy?! He wouldn't tell. So, one night he was followed by two guys down a road. Along came a big truck that passes each night and hits one person, kills him! The other backed away

*in the darkness scared, when here comes the healthy
one with a knife in hand. Cuts open the body, pulls
out the liver, and eats it. Then the heart. My, my, a
man of my OWN. HAHA*

Later,

Art

As an otherworldly note, the following Shawcross
routine, "STUPIDITY," had been inadvertently slipped
into a different envelope than its accompanying letter and
it was essentially lost in the shuffle. Yet the first random
envelope picked out of the pile relevantly contained the
piece. One of several potentially preternatural occurrences
and "coincidences" related to the Shawcross project ever
since it began.

STUPIDITY

*There was this guy out walking the beach one fine
morning very early and he spots what looks like
a bottle sticking halfway into the sand. He sort of
nudges it with a foot and he can see something in it.
He now picks up the bottle and slowly brushes off the
sand, and out pops the cork and three genies. Scared
shitless, the guy drops that bottle and backs up! The
three genies line up and one of them says, "You can
have only one wish from each of us because we are
screw-ups and can't be trusted!"*

*So, the guy thinks a moment. He finally tells the first
genie that he wants twenty naked blondes at his
lodge tomorrow morning. The second genie he looks
and said, "I want 20 million dollars the next day
delivered by the mailman." Then, after pondering for
a time, he whispered his final wish to the third genie.*

Well, lo and behold, the next morning his doorbell rings. When he answered the door, rubbing the sleep from his eyes, there stood 20 naked blondes. He invites them in and fucks all day and all night.

Early the following day, the doorbell rings again. The guy crawls to the door to open it--and there is the mailman with a check for twenty million dollars, which he signs for.

Now he is so tired he'll sleep the rest of the day away.

The next morning, as he gets dressed, there came a POUNDING on his front door. He opens it to see who it could be. There stood three Ku Klux Klan members. He's about to ask what they want when he is suddenly grabbed and dragged out back where he is hung up!

That last genie said to the first, "I understood when the man asked for twenty naked blondes and twenty million dollars. But what I cannot understand is why he wanted to be HUNG LIKE A BLACK MAN?!"

Now don't that beat all. You can smile now you all.

Arthur John Shawcross

* * *

HEY BIG BAD JOHN,

I am way behind in what mail I have in front of me, but I am getting there sooner or later.

I've seen pictures of people jumping off one of the towers. Two people together holding hands and others in single leaps. I guess it all comes down to perspectives of either burning to death or that sudden STOP of hitting concrete! Should have stayed on the roof and rode it down on the fall.

The human can be skinned quite well actually. BUT it tends to SHRINK. So if one does want a skin, one has to find a BIG PERSON to make a coat that would fit. Hahahaha: I can see you now getting one on and can't get it off. Hah Picture that!

I would dry them in powdered sea salt. Bet I could do it for you and it would look nice on you. Hahahaha. Who is the nut here, you or ME? Haha A raincoat with a full pussy or an extra long dick. Ya I am bored too. Haha

I feel quite good at the moment, but I do have a small concern that has been bothering me for a week or so. Pains in the upper right chest area. Either it's a cold or the big one is on the way. Either way I don't give a damn!

I put a new ribbon in this machine and I cannot even erase a mistake. It's a cloth ribbon. I had to wind it up on one of my spools by hand and tape it. But it beats having nothing at all.

My cholesterol count is now 99; and the blood sugar count is at 5.6. Doing good so far in that respect! My temperature was 98.3, a little cool. But good just the same. Hemoglobin was 46% so far. It did get up to 54% at one time. The doctor stated that if it got up to 60% I would have died. How does one know? I asked him if I am considered a mutant?! Haha.

One of the guys came by with a few loaves of white bread and dropped one off with me and it turned out to be moldy. So I complained and got two fresh loaves from the cooler. But I did keep that dead loaf. Took out the moldy ones (slices) and cut up what was left into croutons to dry out. I am always thinking and doing.

I've a chocolate cake mix in from the main kitchen that I will try to bake within a metal hot pot and a tin can. I think it can be done that way. By placing enough oil or grease in the pot and setting the can on top of that. Add the batter and cover at a hot temperature and it just might bake it. Then cut out the bottom of the can and push through. Ya I will try that!

My stepdaughter, Loretta Neal just got home from the hospital after getting a complete hysterectomy to remove a tumor. LUCKY TUMOR to be up in her pussy! Her weight went up to 250 pounds. Not good on a 5'6" frame. Maybe she can start to lose some now.

My fingers are popping the wrong keys at times. I am getting too fast. I had to fix the ribbon again. Son it looks like a never-ending thing.

Try not to ask for a little head from a mixed up genie. Haha You just might get the little head you don't want. Hahahaha

This damn machine!

If you contact NICO again is his email in France or Sweden? I am still waiting to hear back from him. People are funny in the way they come off and promise to do something and you don't hear back from them for quite a while.

I've got to clean up this cell now before the cop comes

by and bitches at me. Be good and take care pal.

Later,

Art

Be good. Indeed. I'm still doing my best, Arthur.

Recently, I was reminiscing about the first person I strangled when I was twelve years old. A kind of Nosferatu nostalgia.

He was a middle school friend, just sitting in the lunchroom waiting for the day's first bell, minding his own business, when a spontaneous shot of adrenaline came over me and I started to squeeze his neck with my small, bare hands from behind him. He was paralyzed as I continued the squeezing for a few seconds until the urge left my body. Robert, another friend of mine across the lunch table, told me that my face had completely changed and was as red as some overly exuberant televangelist. Funny thing is, I was a rather diminutive, usually especially passive boy, and I didn't understand what had come into me. It was a borderline murderous episode--almost like a directed seizure. Having experienced several grand mal seizures and many petite mals from alcohol withdrawals, I'm familiar with the strange sensations that come before and during the seizure, and then the terrifying loss of bodily mechanics right before the blackout comes.

Well, that being said, the kid survived my uncharacteristic onslaught, and somehow, we remained friends. Even if there was some incidental post-traumatic stress that would follow him for the rest of his life.

Yet again, I look to the explanation of black magic giving life to an odd genetic configuration. After the rituals and summoning of...whatever...when I was ten, I used to play--and sometimes believe--that I was possessed by demons. In retrospect, a bizarre alternative to hide-and-seek.

The chokes and strangulations repeated with a few other friends throughout the years, but the methods became more sophisticated as I learned, by way of Jujitsu, the proper and more effective techniques to cut off one's air or blood flow. Personally, I found that cutting off the blood flow to the brain was more merciful for everyone involved.

Shawcross didn't care about mercy, though. My own violence is as peacefully applied as possible. Mostly. One isn't always left with a choice.

Hello John,

I have come to realize that what the military so far in finding Bin Laden is a FARSE! MONEY TALKS... He and his family control too much of the economy! Look at Dow Jones! Their stock is way down. I would buy into them now when the prices are low. Watch what happens when something is being built on the WTC spot. All of a sudden people are buying!!!! Rome is feeling the pinch for real. Too many cocksucking priests and booty bandits! I hope at this moment that Bin Laden is alive to feel every ache he's got.

Where is Maria? Up and gone like so many others! I do not get into it much anymore because of the bullshit.

Nico Claux wrote me and I wrote back. That FUCKER sold my letter for $200 in French money! I hope that fool comes to the STATES: I have a cop waiting on his ass!!!!

150 miles is not far pal. I've done it many times hitchhiking.

A Jewish girl who practices her religion has to be shaved or plucked before marriage. Most likely she is a GRIZZLY otherwise. HAHA But I've seen one that has very little hair! Big nose, big tits, NICE TWAT. In the Arab world women have to be plucked--They stay cleaner that way. NO SAND FLEAS. HAHA Those rules have been around for thousands of years! Any Female Arabs down the street? YA BA DA BA DOO HAHA

There you go--COOK THE COOKS, FEED THE POOR. Make sure you use lots of BBQ sauce.

Maybe someone should wake up the world in this country that everyone came from someplace else. Ancestors, that is. All have equal chances. America is the LAND OF OPPORTUNITY but not for blacks, browns, or tans. HAHA

I've read in THE AMSTERDAM paper that blacks are not allowed an education over 8th grade! A lot of people are pissed off over that!

My wife is doing better now. She is on medication. She was here on the 10th and will be back on the 3rd of August. Clara, my wife, Loretta, my daughter, Lucretia, my granddaughter will be here on the 3rd. Clara is 71, Loretta is 36, and Lucretia is 12. Big girls all around. Loretta may be pregnant. She had her tubes ties 12 years ago, no way she should be pregnant. But a home test says otherwise! I wonder if she can sue the doctor who tied her tubes?!

I sent some sheets + pillow cases to the laundry and they came back smelling like a FRENCH WHOREHOUSE. PERFUMED! Now I have to find out whose clothes were done with mine. Most likely a Miss Thing--HAHA.

I have developed a problem. My right ankle has red blotches all around the leg. Eraser size and they burn. A bit puffy too. I will submit a slip to see the doctor! I hope it does not have to be cut off! Diabetes always starts in the feet! I'll keep you posted on whatever it is.

Later,

Art

Something I noticed during our exchanges, and realize now just how pressing a matter it evidently was, was that Shawcross was continually mentioning how physically ill he was getting. I hadn't paid much attention to this pattern at the time, attributing it to aging in prison, if I gave it any consideration at all. Though, I was deteriorating too. Physically, mentally, and everything in between. My psychotic behaviors were becoming more acute. By now, I'd even added a human skeleton—that I dressed in the suit and tie I'd worn to numerous wakes and funerals before it started to fray a bit--to the inside of the body bag being used as my shower curtain, where it hung for some time. Although, I was stubbornly understanding when one of my sisters was living with me for a while and she replaced the body bag shower curtain with something a bit more conventional--some cheap, trite thing with a number of clearly homosexual fish. But that's what happens when females board your ship. Plus, insult to injury, she accidentally let my uncle's dog in and it ate the bottom half of a shrunken head I'd unfortunately left within the Springer spaniel's reach. My private empire of death was suddenly being dismantled. But everything was, by then anyway.

Hello John,

Man, am I ever sick with the flu bug or something. 16 days of hard breathing! Coughing, sneezing, and chest rattles! All cause by one female teacher. She gave it to her class and then it spread throughout this place!

I've yet to make contact with that so-called fan club in Southern California. Run by a 17 year old! I may have something that group may like. You and I, pal, to fix them up proper. HAHA

All the freaks and geeks have stopped writing in finally. When I don't reply to their bullshit they get the message after a while!

I have people pissed at me because I'll not send anything without a post office box! You send them something and it comes up missing, or so they tell you, but then a week later it turns up on the net! NO MORE!

17 days with a cold now. I sleep sort of at an angle.* Back to bed I go. See you later John.

Art

*Shawcross had included a crude rendering of himself as a stick figure positioned at an angle in his bed.

It has occurred to me that even Shawcross didn't grasp just how scary and off-balance I was getting.

Sitting on a bus or train packed heartily with the most unsuspecting human beings in the world. Could they ever know the monstrosity in their midst? Are there others here like me, I wonder. Although I'm able to keep myself at bay, reserving a wildly amused grin, everyone on the train going on mesmerized by their smart phones or their own daydreams as suddenly the tops of their heads are missing and torrents of blood and cerebrospinal fluid explodes upward like newly-struck oil from each and all of them. On the outside, of course, I'm like them, maybe even appearing like a vaguely productive member of society, as relentlessly brutal music plays remorselessly on my Android. Every one of these strange new friends has become a bleeding fountain carrying on with calm discourse or other preoccupations. There are occasions when I have to hold back a smile, the absurdity of it all so goddamn appealing and spellbinding. The vision is like a farcical Monty Python routine. But they can't see through my eyes and, thankfully (for all of us), can't read my mind, as I'm wondering where the tops of their skulls might be so I can have a full kitchen set of surreal soup and cereal bowls. They're not quite fantasies as much as vividly-projected, turbo-injected suggestions. It's the thought that counts but the hands which collect--and the line to cross is only a footfall away.

Mainly, though, it's most concerning that police agencies and psychiatrists would piss on my parade, considerably diluting any relief I may receive from actually going through with the devilish how-to methods of bringing peace into my life. It's simultaneously why I both need to and CANNOT indiscriminately imbibe shocking amounts of alcohol. The kind of drinking that doctors do spit-takes as though we're in some *Three's Company* slapstick comedy when first glancing at the results of the emergency department admittance urine screen. Heaven forbid my composure is further compromised. When I start thinking about how many pretty heads there are to take home (in a perfect world) on the rare event I have to temporarily integrate or even mingle with society, it's time to sequester myself, soon.

But then, it gets worse and worse. The loneliness brings bitterness and smothering claustrophobia. Socializing, however, reminds me of how much life I've missed out on. I don't understand how people meet and even connect. And while many of them get to enjoy New Sodom and Gomorrah to the fullest, and casually absorb the splendid fuckery of Babylon 2.0, I'm writhing under my covers in a sweat-soaked bed, bargaining with the Devil for an emergency abbreviation of my dumbfounded stay in his wondrous shit show production. The candy may be pretty and delicious, it's just that the poison ruins it. But it goes on for as long as it needs to, like any good screwing.

And so, the secret circus continues.

June 9, 2003

Hey Big Bad John:

I have finally got a stamp to write you back! The knee this day is painful. I think it is due to the weather. I am on MOTRIN for pain. One more rainy day ahead of us. I wish it would stop!

So far Nico Claux has not said a word of what I accused him of or to deny it to the people who will be coming over the interviews. That in itself says a lot of his honesty!

Saddam is still alive and sitting next to Bin Laden somewhere in protection of the good old U.S. of A! No can tell me with all of today's knowledge that we don't know where either of them are!!!!!!!!!! I would sure like to have found that money behind that wall in Iraq! Some servicemen got busted for stealing some of it. They got caught with bags of hundred dollar bills. There was well over a BILLION DOLLARS in that vault behind the wall! It is said that it will be used to rebuild Iraq. BULLSHIT! I bet it gets into SOMEONE'S pockets! One man could not hope to carry all that money away in a very LARGE truck! There was too much of it . Four average size tractor trailers will about do it, but not in ONE!

Ebay is a has-been. There are other websites out there where things can be sold of our nature. One in Canada and another in Europe. Check on it. There is AMAZON, I believe.

So far the New York Post has not written back to me. Why, I don't as of yet know. Because I have two paintings for them to pick up. If they do not acknowledge then I will sell them elsewhere, as I DO have people wanting them! As yet, the story they have has not been published. They are doing research in all I spoke of. I get reporters always asking questions about my past, but not one of them has actually printed what I said! The truth must not be what they really want!

I wish I had a computer in my cell to be able to store and retrieve information when I put it into a book. I do not need one to have outside access, just something like a monitor and printer! The thing is to put one's story in perspective page by page. With a computer you can do just that.

John, EVERY living thing on this planet is future chow for the maggots! We are all going to die sooner or later. I just helped some on their way sooner! If there is a hell, and is all is true about it, then I for sure will not be lonely there because all the people I sent there will be waiting for me to arrive to do it all over again and again! hahaha

Crazy thoughts, don't you agree?!

The difference with a Genesee "Ripper" is that the real ripper sliced up his victims and I did not! A river rat does just about what I did! How about "THE RIVER PHANTOM"? Now THAT has a much better sound to it I think. Smile

Time to close out and get ready for this day ahead. Breakfast is being served.

Until later.

Art

The Shawcross memoirs, with which he recruited me to help him, was in production by 2003, and we were almost immediately having some friendly squabbles over the title. It would go downhill from there.

The Genesee River killer had a certain determination to tell the story of his life and circumstances in his own particular way, from his own point of view, however skewed, self-serving, or misrepresentative that might be. Although when one had committed the sort of crimes that Shawcross had, it would be a bit maudlin to write a book any other way.

It wasn't long before I was able to find a literary agent to represent us after sending several query packages out. That was the good news. The bad news was the agent, excited about the project, had a talk with a publisher over lunch one afternoon and the publisher, while interested, wanted to see the manuscript in its entirety before going any further or green-lighting anything. Apparently, he didn't have much faith in convicted serial killers. But who could one approach for references? Maybe Shawcross (or me, being a complete unknown) would take a cash advance and simply fuck off, he worried, never producing anything but the sample chapters that the subject of the book had provided in good faith. That would've been acceptable for me, but Shawcross was suspicious about handing over everything he had, thinking the publisher might beat him. Besides, the book wasn't even completed yet. I thought the publisher was behaving too hastily. It was all fuckery and reminded me of the drug deals I've been involved in as the buyer, where nobody trusts anyone and it turns into a shit shower. The same would ultimately happen between my friend, Shawcross, and I.

Arthur John Shawcross

9/7/03

POSSIBLE BOOK TITLE: THE BIRTH OF A CANNIBALISTIC MUTANT

MY YOUNG YEARS BETWEEN THE AGES OF FOUR AND NINE WITH INCEST IN THE FAMILY:

YEARS 10 THROUGH 19:

JOBS I HAVE HAD:

GETTING DRAFTED IN THE ARMY:

FIRST TASTE, IF YOU WILL, OF LEARNING TO KILL:

FORT BENNING, GEORGIA:

FORT LEE, VIRGINIA:

23 LEAVE BEFORE HEADING TO VIETNAM:

OAKLAND, CALIFORNIA:

HAWAII:

GUAM:

PHILIPINES:

SAIGON (HO CHI MIN CITY NOW):

VIETNAM:

KOTUMN, VIET, VIETNAM:

DAK TO, VIETNAM:

FIREBASE MARYLOW THREE MILES SOUTH OF KONTUMN:

POLYKLINE FIREBASE:

DRAGON MOUNTAIN, CAMP ENERI, WEST OF

PLEIKU BY SIX MILES:

TEA PLANTATION:

DRAGON'S BEAK-CAMBODIA-LAOS-VIETNAM:

FIRST KILL:

SECOND KILL AND A FEW MORE LATER ON:

CAPTURED ENEMY/KILL:

PATROLS:

CHOPPER FLIGHTS TO A FIRE BASE THAT WAS OVERRUN:

SIGHTS AND SMELLS:

PLANTS AND OTHER THINGS OF INTEREST:

TRAINING MEN TO TAKE MY PLACE SO I COULD GO HOME:

R & R

FLIGHT TO JAPAN; ALASKA; WASHINGTON STATE; CHICAGO, ILLINOIS; SYRACUSE, NEW YORK; WATERTOWN, NEW YORK AND CLAYTON, NEW YORK:

30 DAY LEAVE:

FORT SILL, OKLAHOMA:

DISCHARGED: MY PROUDEST MOMENT TO GET AN HONORABLE DISCHARGE:

DRIVING BACK ACROSS THE COUNTRY:

1969 WENT TO PRISON FOR A BURGLARY I DID NOT COMMIT!:

1972, FIRST MURDER AND ?

THINGS LEARNED IN PRISON AND WHAT I DID NOT LEARN:

RELEASED IN 1987:

BINGHAMPTON, NEW YORK:

JOHNSON CITY, NEW YORK: AT A VESTAL HOTEL:

ELMIRA, NEW YORK:

ROCHESTER, NEW YORK: FIRST YEAR…

1988:

1989:

1990:

COURT AND PRISON FOREVER AND A MOMENT:

IDEAS AND THOUGHTS FOR ANYONE IN PRISON:

PERSONAL THOUGHTS ON ALL MY MISDEEDS:

SIGNATURE:

AJS

* * *

9/7/2003

HI JOHN,

How does this sound to you for starting my life's story? In other words, I have already started and I am on page seven so far. Everything sounds good and I hope it stays that way for the both of us! If you had a phone I could call you now and then if possible, but one can't say much on the phone because it is monitored by the prison!!! I can call you, we can say HELLO COUSIN. Smile

I am whipped and worn out today. I think I have covered about every aspect of my life in the Summary. If you can help me in some way in thinking, it would be ok to lay it on me.

I have been painting things and drawing other things. I have to paint some skulls for a guy in Georgia. Soon to be mailing you the same.

I have to work tonight at the visiting room. Changed re-inked ribbons. I've another letter to write to a female friend that I've known for many, many years inside prison and out! Blonde and furless...hahahaha

Get back to me on what I placed in the Summary. I thank you John. Whenever you get the money some of that you can hang onto for me and bank it somehow. Then when I want an order sent out, all I do is let you know and the order form! How does that sound???

Take care my friend. Take it EEEEEEEEEZZZZZZZZZYYYYYYYYYYY.

LATER,

Art

There are shadows snarling among you.

Imagine, if you will, people affectionately drenched in human blood walking right beside you; strolling just behind you. They are there, you simply don't see them. When one thinks of it, anyone could be one bad day away from being the demon they might've been all along. What kind of demon would you be—would your evil be of finesse or duress? Love can conquer the Beast--for a while--but the default is hate. And hatred nurtures the Beast in habit-forming ways from whence the one who experiences it chooses to not come back. One can become a haven for these energies and entities and he'll feel sapped of power if he doesn't indulge them. Then he deliberately avoids or sabotages any chance to love or be loved. Monsters grow in the dark and, rather like mushrooms, feed on shit, especially the bullshit of daily life.

And I did not need more shit than I was already shoveling into my own trough. Shawcross was putting pressure on me to make things happen that were just not in my control. What I direly needed was for him to be a little more patient with me and the process of publishing. He didn't seem to want to understand that getting anything out onto the market takes time and timing. Not that Shawcross had much time left.

September 21, 2003

Greetings John,

I will go with your choice of number four. Mutant: THE BIRTH OF AN AMERICAN CANNIBAL... ARTHUR J. SHAWCROSS SPEAKS. This one or number three: WHAT YOU DON'T KNOW: THE FULL STORY OF ARTHUR JOHN SHAWCROSS.

* * *

John,

I have at this moment almost 60,000 words down on paper. I have to re-read it and put dates in the sidelines so you can print it all on the computer by the years it happened. I understand what you are asking in the amount of victims domestic. I have been convicted of 12 and suspected of 19. I have also spoke about Jack Blake. I was not convicted of that crime by a deal made by the DA at the time! Do you follow my meaning?!

Memory of some names I do not recall, like people I worked with while in the Army!!! Not one person!!! Now I wish to find out why of that!!! I will not say yes or no to the idea of more bodies in this country. We'll let that stand and the media form their own opinion!!!

When you get the amount offered, send me a copy of what everything is so I can see for myself. I trust you John but it is always better to know too. Do you understand me? Also, my brief has a lot of mistakes in it. I don't have correction on this machine as of yet. When I do I can either correct it myself or let you do it. Since I have done all the hard work so far. Smile.

It would be very nice to be able to be able to order Thanksgiving dinner this year before it gets here. How soon can you find out? I've been too long without!!! A damn shame!!!

No mail in two days. Most likely it will come in on Monday next. I had a man down in Georgia that wanted me to paint him a picture on canvas for only twenty dollars. It cost me $5.99 for the canvas, $5.44 for the shipping and handling. What does that leave me?! SHIT!!! I have been hearing a lot of shit that someone out there is selling my Art work and I want to find out who it is! As it is, I got stiffed by a woman

*over in Gilbert, Arizona for $109.00. I am sending
her name and photo out to someone like me!!! I'll
shut that woman down so she can't get squat!!! Fuck
me. Well, I'll find a way to fuck her and GOOD!!
There is always someone who will do most anything
for you if given the chance!*

*I can hear again. Had to place a new battery in my
hearing aid. Now my overhead light is blinking! What
the heck is next?! If it isn't one thing it's another!!! I
have turned my lamp shade so I can about see what I
am doing. My light bulb is only a 60 watt. It's all we
are allowed anyway. If I had a 150 watt, I could cook
with it! In a day or so that day guy down south is
going to send me a "bitching" letter. Who cares!!!!!!!!
Once we get a good advance, I won't have to depend
on a lot of mail. I can cut down to a few. Maybe less.
But you will always be there John. We have to stay in
contact now.*

I'll go out in the rain and walk.

*We have a man who is always begging for a cigarette
when he knows he can't smoke in his cell! The guards
are waiting to see who gives him one and then give us
both a ticket. Five bucks each!*

*I am always called upon to go that extra mile in
working and this pays off in the long run. I hit my
light switch about forty times and the cop comes by
and asked what is going on. I told him my light blinks
on its own when it wants to, but one of these days
some officer will see to getting it fixed. I have waited
two weeks so far!*

*One of the new men in the shop got arrested for
Rape/Murder and he is always stopping any female
in the hallway and trying to speak to her. The guards*

have already told him to leave the women alone. But he keeps right on doing the shit. Well, today he found himself in a log jam! One female complained and he is in the hole, Segregation, awaiting court. How does a man try to go back to court and still persist in getting messed up with women?! I do not speak to them unless spoken to! But I do say good morning each and every day, and sometimes I tell any of them about a damp or slippery floor if they are going down a certain hallway. This is courtesy for them so I don't get in a jam for getting the floor wet in the first place!

I may have some bad news later this morning. Something to do with my wife! If that is the case I can scratch that and her kids off the list. Maybe not. I'll let you know later.

I was looking for some body powder and couldn't find it and it was right in front of me all the time behind the fan. Crazy, right? We all do this and I wonder WHY at times. Hide things in plain sight and no one can find it. hahahaha

Man, did it ever pour here last evening. The rain came down so damn hard it bounced off the ground. The yards were flooded instantly. People out there got soaked to the skin! I was in the hallway looking out the window laughing at some guys trying to run and then fall in the mud! haha A black man falls in the mud but how do you know if he has mud on him when he looks like mud in the first place? hahahahahaha

So far my co-worker couldn't get a hold of my niece to find out about my wife's status. Sometime today he will try once again. People with answering machines are a pain at times. But most likely they are not home or doing something that they just can't come to the phone at that moment. haha

CHECK YOU OUT LATER PAL.

Art

Shawcross' marriage was falling apart, his health was deteriorating, my health in every conceivable way was deteriorating, and our relationship was becoming uncomfortably unstable. It was only a matter of time. Every relationship I've ever had eventually blew up, came apart at the seams, or was otherwise butchered to bits with no coming back. Nothing new, but always headaches and heartbreaks. Why should my relationship with one of America's most prolific serial killers be any different? Butchery and the general dispensing of life and anything human was, at the end of the night, our bond. Ruin was our destiny.

I got the cheerleader, sure, but only after she'd gained fifty pounds and went insane; I got the hooker, too, but only after she was in abject reform and had given up sex for religion; I got the best friend and secret saint, yes, but he was a minister of rot. And at last, I was freed from police custody, the sheriff and his deputies, the hospitals and doctors, my gruelingly dysfunctional family, alcohol and drugs. But a few paces from it all and I was suddenly in a wasteland stinking like the dumpsite for a hundred holocausts, where digging my own grave in an out of the way corner just feels right. I don't want to die, but I don't want to live. At least Hell was an adventure. This is worse. Much, much worse.

CHAPTER TEN

SAINT ROT

One has the opportunity to flash on a lot of past dramas whenever shackled in the back of the sheriff's department transport van—the rolling dog kennel. I'd be transfixed on everything and anything I could see through the rear window, riding through what I now considered an unreachable paradise as an invisible prisoner, feeling a glow come over me with every tree or restaurant we passed. I made pained effort to imprint the sights of these wonderfully normal things and the outer home from which I'd been removed, before the D.O.C. stowed me away in their bleak caverns of gray just up ahead but not in the world. Resistance is brutal. Such has been the situation for me on several occasions over the years, interspersed between bouts of drunken terror, societal menace, and droning aimlessness with interludes of suicide-inducing monotony.

Things like the family tree come into question. The Fay name is on the George Bush family tree and the real Dracula, Vlad Tepes, is on that very same tree. Considering this, certain things seem to fall into place. Since I was a child, I've been compared--affectionately, for the most part--in some ways to Dracula. Even a certain female mental health worker I'd grown close to, through the course of the program assigned to me through probation, respectfully mentioned that I had a "Dracula-esque" way about me. It's apparent that I've, indeed, been known to have a vampiric vibe. There is an ongoing background of flashbacks of blood-laced rum cocktails and the occasional red room that my ivory bunker had at times become. The blood-encrusted place stinking of copper or rust the mornings after my self-fulfilling prophecies of ritual gore, and a random insurance company's wall calendar, a different decapitated head drawn by me into every day of the month. I wasn't sure how relevant the heads were to my schedule. Maybe more relevant than I wanted to consider.

HI JOHN:

Who is fucking pumpkins NOW? Haha Happy Halloween to you also. I wish I had about 50 lbs of Halloween candy right now but I am not supposed to eat it unless it is pure chocolate. But I have some coming in anyway.

I knew that there was more than one shooter in that DC deal! I was asked in here by some of the guards my view on this and that is what I told them. Now they come back and ask how did I know?! I used logic! That white van was a ploy! They parked next to white vans to shoot people! Well now they will be going to court for a while in different states and then die!!!!!!! CRISPY CRITTERS THEY WILL BE FOR SURE!

I have been up close and personal and I have shot people from a quarter mile away too. But I did that in Vietnam only. I did have thoughts of shooting DRUG DEALERS on street corners from as far away as possible. Hit them low! Would I do that shit? You damn betcha I would! Hahahaha

I've never ate a cat as in a house cat, but I have eaten puma, mountain lion. I have chewed on some Chinese girls before. Kind of skinny though. But some are quite nice when fed right. Smile

If you email to Nico's website, tell him that I am looking.

I am interested in that book you describe about the Zodiac serial killer. What will someone think of next?!

I got in a few catalogs last evening from DICK BLICK. Thanks. This is the first time that a company has sent any type of catalog to me. One does get pissed off when he needs things. I've got that BILLION DOLLAR BILL in my wallet now. My boss offered me a two dollar bill for it. Like that would impress me. Novelty bills sound ok. I have one with Monica Lewinski.

John, I have a tumor under my right arm in the center of my armpit. It hurts now and then. I have an appointment for next week to see the doctor. There is no way that QUACK is going to play with this!!!! I will be sent up to Albany Medical for the operation and brought back. I am not too happy over it!

I am heading off to work now and the rest of the afternoon I'll be in the gym, stripping a small hallway.

Fuck a ROBOT only if it has parts soft enough. Hahahaha. Take a bath to get a blow dry job hahahahahahahaha

Take it easy pal. See you later.

Art

In 2002, and into 2003, back when banks still believed in my ability to continue payments on my loans, I traveled out to Mesa, Arizona, near Phoenix, to invest in a low-budget horror comedy movie called "Blown." It was basically about a blowup sex doll which becomes possessed by the spirit of an accidentally murdered witch who seeks vengeance. Not something that I had, nor would I have, written but decided that it would at least be an interesting investment, afford me some exposure, and I could escape the New England winter for a few weeks. Throughout my stay there, I continued seamlessly with corresponding to Shawcross. The timing was ideal for getting away from Boston not only because of the horrendous winter that it was about to undergo but I'd put myself well on the radar of the mental health community when I showed up to my maiden appointment with a therapist drunk on rum and stoned on oxycodone. It wasn't ten minutes into our talk, as I was sitting across from the pretty young woman, quietly admiring the sexiness of her boots, when she called security to try to have me locked up in an involuntary treatment program.

Thankfully, that was one I was able to talk my way out of. But it got me back to thinking of making voodoo dolls of my therapists. I once made one as a quasi-playful gesture of a favorite therapist up to that point, Jennifer, who I also asked out on a date a couple of sessions in. She was tactful in turning me down. Hence, the voodoo representation. Jennifer wasn't quite sure what to make of it when I showed her the doll during one session. She asked if I was trying to scare her. Perhaps she was scared but I don't feel that it was the exclusive intention. I much would have preferred turning her into a mindless slave than having her scared of me. I just think that everyone should have a voodoo doll of his therapist, significant other, etc., to keep things as fair as possible. That's my philosophy.

Shawcross references the murder-suicide of my aunt's former tenants in one of the Mesa letters. He wondered why the case hadn't made national news. It made the local news of course, but it got me thinking as to how common the mass murder of one's family had become. He suggested, as to motive, that the husband had simply been fed up with life on life's terms. Overall, a truly dystopian future unfolding. But I too kept a weirdly cozy corner in it, where I had my own sleaze weasels to tend to. And I wasn't just living in sin, I was the mayor of it.

JANUARY 5, 2003

HAPPY NEW YEAR JOHN

John:

Well here it is a new year ahead of us and we are still doing the best we are able. Mesa, Arizona. Sounds like a hot dry place to be. See any UFOs out that way lately? Tell me you're not going crazy pal over a blowup doll?! It sounds like a horror comedy type of film. What is the budget of the film? It's not written as yet. Shit! How about getting me to help the doll get into the gruesome aspect of the film? Haha I guess you need a bit of animation with a computer to get a blowup doll to perform.

What's going down with that guy who killed his whole family? How come it didn't reach national news? My thoughts are the guy was fed up with the bullshit!

We got hit with one hell of a snowstorm here yesterday pal. 16 inches of blowing snow. Cold too. If you flew from Boston to Mesa it had to be about three hours or less. There is a plane now that can go around the world in less than an hour and a half! But it blew out an engine on the test flight. smile: haha I think I would enjoy it more driving out there from home! When I drove from the Thousand Island area of New York State back in 68, it took me 23 hours to do so. But when I came back it took only 19 hours driving. Nonstop, other than gas and food.

My tumor is going down for some reason. It puffed up but broke the surface and drained out some pretty strange looking liquid. The doctor didn't think much of it so what am I to do to but leave it be!

The latest news is as usual: broke and trying to get my head above the surface of the road I fell on! Where can I find a sponsor for my Art Work? I hear a new law passed in Arizona and it is retroactive across the country. Concerning artwork by inmates. It's called Freedom of Expression. Freedom of Speech we did not lose! So this was given back to us. Maybe I can start painting for real this time. I am practicing on my sketches.

SADDAM is one tough SON OF A BITCH! He will be forced to bring out his bio weapons when the military gets on the rush toward his ass!!!! I would say by March or April the jump off time Bush will send in his troops. They are gearing up for the real thing this time for sure! Men and women troops are set up to go in. But check this out John: The Iraq people have teenagers fighting now too. Catch one or two female prisoners and make them dance to the tune of you know what! hahaha Fuck them where they breathe. But don't get caught by them bitches or you might be ball-less! haha

Last evening there was a fight in here that was quite a bit entertaining. One Spanish guy and a Black. The Black got his little ass kicked for real. But not one guard seen a thing. The inmates blocked the view of it. But the black went to his cell at lock-in and has not come out since. My thoughts are this guy will come out with a blade! Or the other one will!

NO ONE IS GOING TO MAKE A MOVIE ON MY

LIFE FOR FREE! I'll not give out the ok! Fix up my wife and we can talk...

Let me make my own film and you can scare people for real! Haha I'd have to sit down and talk this over with a lawyer first. Sorry.

Thanksgiving was ok and for Christmas I got nothing from anyone, not even my wife!

For New Year's day I made five cheesecakes. I made my own cream cheese. It takes me about 22 hours to make half a pint of cream cheese from two quarts of milk. Doesn't sound like much but given that amount each day mounts up after a week. I have one on the heater now working. I'll get cheese by 5AM tomorrow morning.

Any Martian who abducted Maria needs saving. hahaha

She is stuck on bullshit! Why couldn't that woman just come to see me before she jumped in front of the train with her baby. I would have fixed her right proper without danger to the kid. I guess she had no one to love her or help her in her daily needs. It is bad near Christmas or New Year for some people. A person getting run over by a train is QUITE A MESS. One can only hope they died quick and didn't suffer for long. Shit, I'VE carved up a few bodies in my day and it DOES NOT COMPARE TO A TRAIN!

Picture you with a pet scorpion out there in the desert. Trim its stinger though. Haha Better to have ANY companionship than none with no actual friends in all of Arizona as you say. Pull yourself together pal. Haha

I will close now and get some much needed rest before something unexpected goes on. Keep me posted on your endeavor of this blowup doll. smile: Have you used one yet? Just don't fall in love with those things. They'll leave you FLAT! haha

LATER,

Art

In the dream, I watch myself taking a jaunt through the woods where I had to live for several months. It seems like a relaxed run and then farther outside of myself, I realize that I'm running on railroad tracks. The jog goes on calmly and then I see just up ahead the commuter train coming. I'm unfazed, seeming to have embraced what's coming and timed the arrival perfectly. As my body collides with the train, the world turns red. The sky bleeds giant blood drops and rains an army of falling angels. I see my whole life play past my eyes. Not just a dream but a recurring theme. I find myself right in the arms of Lucifer.

(A four-leaf clover was Scotch-taped above this letter's heading. --JPF)

Hi John,

I must be losing my mind. Here I sit looking for your letter and it's right in front of me! I better leave the cunt alone. HAHA Thanks for the m.o. pal. I sure needed it!

My wife is ready to check out and that hurts deep within me. But if that is the case, I'll get another. Can't keep a good man down! But I have one in mind. She lives in upper Maine. 24 year old Blonde. But fat though. WHO CARES AT MY AGE?!!!! She has a waxed, bald cat. Smile I would have married Maria but she is too far away! Most everyone I know lives far away. But I have had a visit that will last me a while, man! A local gal came in to spend a day with me. What a KNOCKOUT! Blonde. Miniskirt, crotchless panties. Flavorable too. Tasted like cherry. HaHa Like KENTUCKY FRIED CHICKEN -- Finger lickin' good...Slurrrrrp HAHA Ya man, I sure did. She slid her hand down my pants and I exploded. I wonder what she did with it, as she closed her fist and went to the bathroom. Most likely swallowed it. HAHA Her tits were a mouthful. We took two photos together. One for me and one for her. Guess what John? She will be back in about a week. Hardly any fuzz on her box. Felt good though. Smile

I wonder what local people think about eating pork of pigs that ate humans? HAHA Eat me babe: HAHAHAHAHAHA

Been there, did that!

I've given you Maria's mother's home address , or "mum," as she says it. Maria had to move out of the flat because her landlady was selling the building.

I read the same thing as you on 9/11 by the way. Yes, Big Ben in London was supposedly another target- -Parliament and the Queen. Paris--the Tower. But it did not come about, did it?! Maybe BULLSHIT spread by the government! Planes in this area have a different route. We get a lot of jets flying over here! That dirty bomb is bullshit too! SCARE TACTICS by Uncle!!!! Israel will get a dirty bomb before anyone else...Bet on it.

Be good now

Or

B-good at it.

Later,

Art

Shawcross was not alone in perceiving a further cracking of his sanity.

I couldn't stop, for the life of me, getting thrown out of places and, then, inconvenienced by layovers in jails or being committed by family members for drunken messes. I was fortunate to have been assigned some lovely public defenders going above and beyond for me.

The final time that I was removed from the bunker, jailed until the Massachusetts Bail Fund came through with the $500 bail, I had to return to retrieve some personal items, especially my eyeglasses, which I had been without for nearly two weeks by that time. I arrived with two police officers accompanying me. I went through the proper channels this time, having already violated the restraining order and facing two-and-a-half years in the House of Corrections for it. Now, dear Uncle Jerry, asked venomously in front of the officers, "How'd you get out of jail?" Doing what I could to collect everything I needed as quickly as possible, I distractedly explained about the jail fund. Then, all of a sudden, he took out one of the boxes I had some of my things stored in and began displaying to the cops the death scene photos, letters from Shawcross, and whatever else he could to even further damn me. It was vile and deliberately meant to cause me even more problems. As if I hadn't had enough, essentially homeless now, with scarcely any money, and a two-and-a-half-year sentence hanging over me and this overgrown, grossly dimwitted child, just won't stop saying stupid things as I'm scrambling around trying to find clean underwear.

It seemed he was still having a tantrum over me finding out, by going up to Boston City Hall, that Auntie Lorraine had left my sisters and me part of the house, and we weren't supposed to know. But somehow, he and certain cousins had killed that will, so to speak. Is it really any wonder that I exploded on these people? I scoffed at "stop resisting." START resisting! I'm stuffing things into plastic bags and the wonderful Uncle Jerry is introducing the officers into a part of my world not meant to be seen--especially by the POLICE! The officer with Jerry said something like, "We might have to take him in." That was when I hurried myself out, hoping that the cop with me hadn't heard what his partner had just been considering. Apparently, he had not and I felt that it was yet another close call.

Then as mentally disheveled as I was, after I got out of there, I realized that I'd left all my debit cards and money behind. Funny, I gathered all the Shawcross correspondence and artwork but it wouldn't suffice for train fare. I'm a believer that things happen for a reason, though, as evidenced by this account. With the police escorts gone, and me not about to call on them again, I was lost. I regretted not being able to take the near-full half gallon of rum that was right on the dresser. I tried to take it but Jerry thwarted my effort to stuff the bottle into a bag. A spite move more than looking out for my well-being, which was ostensibly his reasoning. The officer standing by certainly didn't mind that I wanted to take it. Oh, boy, though, I was ready to drink.

Thankfully, due to my sister talking our awesome father into letting me stay at the dollhouse for a while, I, regrettably, had to go back there. All I needed was the train fare--which I didn't have. Throughout all of this, I was running around with a half-shaven face, my random Islamic jail barber not getting the chance to complete his work when the C.O. called me to let me know that I was getting bailed. Already I was labeled a maniac and this hardly helped! Somehow, through a strange and circuitous route, a half-soused lady at the local yacht club donated twenty dollars, just to get me out of the yacht club, I imagine. That was enough to get me where I needed to go. But I couldn't believe it: I was heading back to the dollhouse--and my father! How wasn't this going to be another series of tragic events?

Hey John,

You got "BLOWN AGAIN" haha: Crazy man!

Hey, what's new in the Northeast? I hear one of yours is dead from freezing a Korean War Veteran. A shame he had to die like that! It is said that you go to sleep in the freezing cold and don't wake up. No pain at all. Just dreamland! Wild shit, that! I got a new gal pal from Johnson City, New York. She is within two hours of here. Cool: Maybe I can get a visit or three this year from this one. She is all of five foot tall and soaking wet at a hundred pounds. I think she is nice with her 34C tits. Haha I have one over in England who wants to come over and stay with my wife and they both come down. No no no: haha That just will not do at all! I had written and told my wife about all the women who write in. Just in case she came in and one of them was visiting. I told her I get more mail from other guys' wives than my own wife!

This woman in Austria wants me to tie her up tight and fuck the living shit out of her. No good at all. She is teaching her 10 year old daughter the tricks of self satisfaction with rope and leather. Two FREAKS for sure! When the daughter gets to be about 14 or 15, THEN I will teach her a thing or three!!! Hahahahahahahahahahahahaha Momma too and all the neighbors at that!

An everyday UFO is a dust mote, flying through the air in here. You wonder how we humans can breathe through this shit. You only see it when the sun comes in a window just right. Pat the couch or a soft chair and see the dust in the air. Now that I think of it I see where my nose gets stuffed up so much. Without the nose hairs we would die! I'd much rather sniff pussy motes: hahahahahaha

John, we busted a new record for this area in cold weather this past three weeks! Last night it got down to 32 below with wind chill factor! There just may be another ice age coming soon. I can take it I think. Frozen pussy is not too bad. Been there pal: Eat it frozen and it is pretty good. First you shave the hair off, then it's BITE SIZE. Hahahaha

I caught a contract to paint a few paintings for an inmate. He ordered two hundred dollars worth of supplies for me. Now I can get started again. I have three orders set on the desk ready to go. One is for $145.00; another is for $201.00; and the third is for $234.94! I will get it yet!

I turned that woman loose up in Maine. I have not heard from her in two months. So I gave her name and address to a black dude, plus all of her photos. He was very happy to get them. Hope he gets her to write to him, the little pervert! Hahahaha That gal in England wants to rape me. So does the one in Johnson City, N.Y.

Count Time, back later.

What is it with these women? I would bet they would shit if I knocked at their doors! Women like this only dream of doing it and not for real.

It is about 4 pm at the moment. Men are coming in from the yard and other programs. I have the day off and tomorrow as well. But I'll say this much, I had a good sleep this afternoon!

Can you picture John that a few NUKES dropped on the USA and you and I had to revive the women and girls by fucking them. Now that may be a good idea! But I would hit the drug stores for all the testing boxes I came across. I'd be doing my DAMN BEST to revive quite a lot of them. Hahahahahahaha I figure by giving them a good stroking they would start to wake up. Slave market for sure. Because they would need at least a hundred to be fully awake. Smile: Now you get the idea. We can always toast some of the bad ones for candles.

Iraq sponsored executions. Now that would not sit well with some people. But for kids growing up and into all kinds of shit, it might really get their attention for sure! It might be a sort of film to show at a party to get the women breathing heavy. Hahahaha I've seen some of what goes on in some Arab countries in killing and cutting off the hands and arms as well. If caught as a thief, you lose a hand. BOTH hands if again. A THIRD time and you are dead!!!!! Shrink their heads so they get the message!

As for doing a story (book) and movie of my life it would cost at least $750,000. I would say that this film and book would be one hell of a story!

NOW HEAR THIS: Some guy was arrested for SCREWING A SHEEP! hahaha He claimed that the sheep had no AIDS! Its first time! Hahahahahahaha I don't know any more, do you? Over in England a man was caught by his wife sitting on the couch naked except for one of her blouses and nylon stockings on fucking a frozen turkey. She screamed at him that the turkey was her Sunday lunch. He said they can still eat it. hahahaha hahahaha She kicked his sorry ass out the door and filed for divorce! Now why did he grab a frozen turkey? Maybe he pretended that the turkey was his wife: smile Makes for a good laugh.

NEWS NEWS NEWS NEWS NEWS NEWS NEWS NEWS NEWS NEWS NEWS NEWS

Maria is back again. Contact her at her old address. Left her boyfriend finally.

I am still trying to get a copy of this Freedom of Expression thing. As yet, the library has not got it in. Soon.

Play the lottery John. I have to find a way to get a painting out to you. Be good.

Later,

Art

The darkness that comes after certain storms can be emotionally crippling. Though I got along infamously with Arthur Shawcross, that wasn't necessarily the case with blood relatives so much. I was only permitted to stay back at the dollhouse temporarily after what amounted to paying a form of "protection" to my father. That and the assurance of not drinking. I at least kept up the financial end of the bargain.

Ever compounding the misery, it was a house full of people and only a single bathroom while I was accustomed to having a private bathroom of my own, which is a luxury that I'll never again take for granted. I mostly sequestered myself in the cramped upstairs room where I was staying, sinking deeper into a swamp of shit and I soon fell back into a secretive drunkard's charade. Dreading to see anyone else in that house, I resorted to urinating into empty apple juice bottles, which I shoved under the bed, often forgetting to dump them into the toilet for days.

One particularly sad day after I'd just had a heartfelt discussion with my court-appointed attorney--who was the closest I had to a therapist at the time--I had about a shot and a half of rum left and just enough apple juice to mix a drink before I could muster the energy and wherewithal to go out on a mission to the liquor store for another bottle of Bacardi. It was a mentally fogged up day and I was feeling a bit woozy after the subterfuge boozing from the day and night before. I thought I'd run out of apple juice, which is what I was making the drinks with, but was somberly pleased to see that I, in fact, had not.

I knew there hadn't been any apple juice left. I KNEW it. It was simply a bad case of denial and drunken logic.

Desperately, I took in the first gulp of that dire drink, and then realized that having had just enough juice left for the cocktail was one of those things that was just way too good to be true. I held the mouthful, fighting to will myself to pick up the vaguest flavor of apple juice but, for certain now, it was all the warmest and most wretched piss and, worse, the last of the rum. However, being the alcoholic I was, and, besides that, it being the end of the bottle, I tried to psych myself up into just getting that bit down and it'd be over with. There I sat on the floor with *I Dream of Jeannie* playing on the classics lineup on TV, the windows covered with makeshift curtains to keep the daylight out, and then me, gagging, eyes tearing, and in near-death need of a buzz while Jeannie was blinking up some more misguided magic. I thought, well, there are people who drink their pee, right? Isn't it supposed to have healing properties or something? Or is that whole thing a mockery scam? Anyway, at least it's MY urine! Even if all of that healing urine trend may've been true, I'm sure the concept didn't apply to two-day-old stagnant piss sitting in a plastic bottle in a stuffy room tucked halfway under a bed somewhere in Fucksville. I almost got it down. It wouldn't hold, though. And I did fight to keep it in with whatever I had left, but in the end, it was another session of projectile vomiting into a plastic bag that I hoped didn't have holes in it. The worst of it really was the waste of liquor, and that actually was how I felt about it. At least I had the bag handy. That wasn't always such an available nicety.

I was struggling anti-heroically to evade sobriety. Sober equals pain. That's when I nitpick and needle nose plier the smallest details of everything that could've or should've been different. Could I have also played the Shawcross hand differently? I wasn't so sure one way or the other. What I did know was that our relationship was falling apart fast.

Hello John:

It is better late than never; no stamps nor the money at the time for any. But I borrowed. I just tore up a letter from a HOLLAND man. I didn't like that way he came off to me! Bragging on all the other people he is in contact with and the names of same. THAT I did not need in my life. I am not a THING. I am a ME, MYSELF AND I. Ah, shit. Hahahahahaha

Frozen pussy IS nice to nibble on! One does not need teeth to eat a frozen pussy! I do just fine with what I have. I eat all kinds of things without any teeth. Nuts, twigs and chicken bones. I can crunch potato chips with the best of them!

Some asshole came up to me and asked what I did with a head in a box. I told him to ask his Mother. He got pissed off and I just stood there and smiled. Like what am I to do with a stupid question of which I know nothing about?! I told him that he had the wrong man for that shit! Another guy came up and started to ask a question and I put a stop to it. I don't know who he is putting out anything about a head in a box! The second guy said that was not you! Then I told him to tell this fuck that he did but the guy was still pissed for some odd reason about asking his mother. Then I said FUCK YOUR MOTHER! How's that, I said! I really wanted to hit this man and hurt him. I turned and started to walk away and the guy slugged me in the back of my head. I stopped and turned around and said, does your sister fuck too? That brought the response I wanted. Without reason he charged at me; one to the throat and down he went. Sleep that off you fuck! I took his pants off and tied his ankles together. Laid him belly down on his bed! Hahahaha I get strange looks from this guy now. Haha Think what you want guy. Hahahaha

I have a key sticking on this machine. My Shift key. I need a bit of WD-40 to loosen up something. Maybe I will take it apart and clean everything under the keys. I've a meeting this evening. I am voted in as Secretary for the Veterans Office for a year. I take down what is said in minutes in all meetings. I even add what is voted on in a special log book. So it is mandatory that I be there.

Dust in the air is dead skin of people. How nice. There is a lot of NEAR DEAD in this place! Haha

Quite a few men are being sent elsewhere. Due to the massive search of this place, several men got caught doing things that were against the rules. Several items such as tin can lids that are sharpened; and several pieces of Plexiglass sharpened to a razor edge were found in the Law Library no less. Also in the Law Library there are clerks that were extorting guys to help do their law work. Well they got caught and are being shipped out! All the good guys are gone! Even though they were a real pain in the ass so to say!

That Jonson City woman did respond back to me.

Maybe it was not a woman in the first place. That is how I catch on when they don't live far away. They ask me things and I tell them to come for a visit and I never hear back. Pure Bullshit!

I fixed that damn key with a tiny drop of 3-in-1 oil. I have a little musk oil tube of it and it sure comes in handy. The keys with the A & S on them are faded to halfway gone. I repainted them but they are worn off again. I'll find me some small letters that stick on the keys. A little dab will do ya. Hahahaha

I would love to tackle a woman with her naval pierced! Bet she would go wherever I lead her if I tied something to the little bars. Hahahaha Car battery hookup, zap zap. One for the clit too. Hahahaha

Many of these women get a bunch of shocks when they get a knock at their door and someone says: Greetings from Lord Arthur. Hahahaha I would surely love to be able to knock at every one of these women's doors and see just what kind of reaction they give up. I bet there are several that will pull me in and fuck my brains out right there upon the floor by the door! Smile: Hey man, it's worth the thought, isn't it?

John, why don't you write Maria direct and ask for her email if she has one or a new one. I have been waiting for her to write back. That English woman is a trip! She ever comes back and I will sue her ass for real. She didn't honor her contract with me! I wrote to the TV station and they said what you had with Ms. English was her business. So she was acting alone it seems! Next time I see her I just may take a bite out of crime! hahahaha hahahaha

In my next life I will be better than I am now, that's

for sure. I'll be a hunter: A keeper of many!

I may not have heard back on this so-called Freedom of Expression but I am able to sell my Art work direct from here to whomever wants it. They are looking the other way sort of. Keep the publicity down is what they really want!

If North Korea want to hit the Northwest with a nuke they will be committing death unto themselves for damn sure!!!!!!!!!!!!!!!! They can hit any American air base in South Korea if they so choose. That will get them wiped out too.

Another ribbon shot to hell.

It's not that the Space Program is pushed back, it is the maintenance problem that does not get done on the shuttles. Make sure all is well before sending one up! Use something long enough and don't maintain, then you run into problems for a fact! The United Nations made the Moon off limits for a space station. Because then it becomes property. You can sell the Moon to anyone then! Just like Prudential: A PIECE OF THE ROCK: hahahaha

LATER PAL.

Art

* * *

Hello John,

I have been in the hospital for an injured left knee and leg. Man I am so drugged up I feel no pain. At the moment I am back in my cell. Two months of hell!

I still don't know how I hurt my leg!

I've not done any painting in some time John. Right now my leg is propped up and damn near upside down that I am. Once back on my feet I may get into something. Art supplies have been ordered. Some of them anyway. I've got four more orders to get out yet. I've another company in England asking for an interview on my art work. Nico Claux is supposed to be with them as an extra camera man! But I put a bee in their minds on Nico. He did not keep his word with me concerning art supplies! I may have told you, I don't remember. He said he would send me all the art supplies I'll ever need: Right, sure, LIAR! But I informed this woman to make me an offer I can't refuse! Think they will bite?

Bombing Iraq is over more or less. Now that Saddam is not there, ALL HELL BREAKS LOOSE WITH THE PEOPLE! They want us gone! Not likely: THEY are the conquered people. Did you check out on the news where all those millions of dollars were found inside a wall at a Saddam palace? All one hundred dollar untraceable bills. Needed a huge truck to carry it all. With that amount of money every Iraqi civilian could share of it. But watch where that money goes!

So where is Saddam and his sons, killed or stolen away? Another Bin Laden trick, ESCAPED...

OH, if I get my hands on that English woman, I'll fuck up her own little world!!!!! She may not know anything afterwards. HAHA Maria is a trip -- she ALSO needs to be fucked hard for several days + nights!

"WOMEN," John, I get lots of mail from women. Some normal, some hot + sexy, some freaks, and a

few who want to be my wife. I'll take them all. HAHA One woman is a good 400 LBS. HAHA FAT AND SASSY. Does not get fucked, I'm sure! Top that off, I get a fag now and then posing as a woman! Sooner or later they make a mistake! They want to blow me, HAHA, yah right, sure, everyday—

NO FUCKING WAY MAN!

I've got photos like you would not believe! These women only write to ME, NO ONE ELSE. Some letters are soaked with perfume pal. Love it.

The Freedom of Expression Act is in. I can sell, trade, or give all my Art work, poems, and whatever to whomever I choose. Now that Ebay does not sell inmate art anymore.

This morning I was on an exercise bike that the handles that move as well. I DANG NEAR FELL OFF THAT MACHINE. Then when I did come off I was given two rubber paddles stuck to my knee, wrapped in heavy rubber and a towel. The machine it was hooked up to gave heat to my leg, plus small shocks of electricity. Another hour I pop another pill.

I mayonnaise my face. Everything else does not seem to work to keep my dry skin moist. I even use it in my hair when I shower sitting in a chair. HAHA Just call me the CRIPPLE!

There are some new cards out now calling me the River Rat. Whatever. I can't control that shit! The New York Post newspaper will soon do something on me. I have a letter stating so. More publicity, more mail! I am not a rat's rat though -- I don't squeal on anyone!

I've gotten two books from a BIKER MAMMA North of you in New Hampshire in Belmont. She is 6 foot tall, 210 LBS and 80% of her body is tattooed, plus pierced everywhere many times over! If she took out her earrings her ears would whistle in the wind. HAHA But if you spread her legs it gets SCARY! She has a ring in 14 places on her cunt -- one barbell on her clit. Check this out John -- she has shaved her head on one side -- NO PUSSY HAIR THOUGH. Picture that going through an AIRPORT: HAHA A REAL TRIP MAN! I bet she gives a good BLOW JOB! Nose pins + rings and chin ball. A bar on the tongue too. So how does one chew their food? SWALLOW IT BABY: HAHA It wouldn't take much makeup to make her scary at all. On one side of her head she has hair to her mid-back.

Soup time + Jello. Forced to lose weight.

If Uncle George had kept that gold he would have been rich. Me too! I did the same. If I had of mined some gold in Laos, let's say, I'd be rich today or DEAD.

One of my friends is locked up. Being out of place. He escorts the blind. Instead of coming back to the block, he went to speak to his Boss. Can't do that without telling someone!

Well my friend, I shall close for now. When does your film come out -- I'd like to see it. It's GOT to be FUNNY!

Later,

Art

* * *

Hey John:

What is kicking? I have been on vacation of sorts with the mail. Now I know what David Berkowitz has gone through! He does not write to very many people. He rips up all his mail and keeps what he wants. He is no more the "Son of Hope" than I am!

I am now called THE MUTANT: Even the guards are calling me that. It is better than being called Hannibal the you know what! Haha Some people just have no sense of humor!

My interview with 48 Hours was a flop! I got pissed off when I went into it at first because there sat DIANE SAWYER! I gave permission to be interviewed by DEBORAH GRAU only! I called the woman a bitch on camera and she agreed. Question John: How can someone or anyone remember what they said 13 years ago? This bitch asked me things I can't recall! It was total bullshit...No tit to speak of and too damn thin for me. I will say she has a throat that will take a good dick. Hahahaha One of those long necks to cut very easy with a big blade, CHOP...

Ms. Sawyer asked me if I had had sex with a dead body and if so how did it feel?! I came back and asked her if she would like to find out...haha Fuck that bitch. She said that she will have to go with what is public knowledge and I came back with: that was what you were going to use in the first place, were you not?! She agreed! Stupid cunt! What I would like to have done with her can't be placed in print... She'd be well fucked coming and going every hole she has! Smile: WOULD I DO THAT? Haha You bet your booty I would.

The Fourth of July I went to the veteran's office and

had lunch with several other vets. It beat what was served outside in the yard! I did like Hot Dogs! We don't get real hamburgers here but some sort of soy burgers. I won't eat that either!

My story is worth at least $50,000! I will have that placed in several banks. Or buy my wife a real home other than a trailer! I will not do this cheaply!!

I see more Americans are getting killed in Iraq! Why does not the soldiers go in and remove every weapon from the whole country!!!

I would just drop a nuke on them to play with if they lived…

That Stephen King story, any man who is stranded on an island and can't survive without eating himself is better off dead! I, my man, would be healthy for sure! Bet on it! There are too many fish, clams, birds and eggs to be had to eat your own dick. Haha But what does a doctor know about survival?!

I ripped one bitch open. JUNE STOTTS. She was a very good fuck if you ask me. She kissed me everywhere and did me everywhere! Quite a gal even if she was a retard of sorts. Oh well, she is history and cannot come back again. When I did and go to hell she will be waiting there for me to do it all over again. Good theory, haha.

I will end here and get something to eat. A sandwich maybe.

Take it easy or take it twice.

LATER,

Art

* * *

HI JOHN,

What is the term "obscenely short"? haha Only
kidding you.

THE BIG BLACKOUT OF 2003 was a washout.
Not much went on in this area of the state! People
just took it in stride. Now the electric companies are
going to charge the people so they can pay for the
repair of the lines. Now that is not fair at all! I was
surprised that it came out of Ohio! The last one came
out of Canada. Now being stuck in an elevator might
be quite pleasant if, let's say, a bunch of women are
on there. Someone will just have to pee. Hahahaha
I would like that to be stuck in an elevator with a
bunch of women and me the only man. I can feel
things without anyone seeing me do it. Smile

This new sniper is another nut case, but this one has
a mad-on for cops. A green pickup is looked for. But
this time the cops have not said what type of gun
is killing people! I think it is better that way! Fuck
a bunch of Mexicans!!!!!!!! I got a mad-on for that
tribe!

Diane Sawyer came on like GANGBUSTERS! I
backed off right away. She got stuck on trying to find
out about Jack Blake. I cannot say anything about
that as I was not charged with the killing! I told this
bitch that and she just could not accept the statement
that I will not discuss the issue! I made an agreement
with Deborah Grau for an interview and she got this
bitch to do it instead of herself. It was WAY out of
line! I didn't say much of anything. Then got up and

left. Ms. Grau was pissed for sure! A wasted trip! Fuck them all!

The English woman may try to get here in November yet. She was sent to a hospital for an operation. I am trying to locate her as I type this letter. If I had sex with Ms. Sawyer I bet it would be like fucking a dead body. Haha Oh well, fuck it while it's still warm, as they say. How many MORTICIANS have done just that while they are still warm. Smile

If a publisher thought they was finally going to get a book about my life they would jump at the chance if they were serious! I am not that stupid! You get me $25,000 John and you get the other $25,000! Or more, we split it! If that is agreeable then let's get with the program. I'll tell you what to do with my end of the money. Royalties will go to whomever I choose if this is agreeable too. I could ask for it to be banked in my name at that! John, I will put stuff in this book that has not been written about me anywhere. Shit, that was left out on purpose from my so-called family! They have not spoken to me in many years. Mom and Dad since 1987! Everyone else since 1972! I gave all the information to Jack Olsen but even he did not put anything I said in his book! But I have proof he did send money to me for that information! I got $300 in one shot and a hundred a month afterwards. That kept me going for a while.

I will write this book year by year as I can remember. That is the proper way to get it done. I will start when I was born and work forward on information until I can bring my own memory of what I did and I mean EVERYTHING I did! No punches pulled...

Matter of fact, I will send you in this letter an

envelope that Jack Olsen sent me a hundred in. I'll keep the rest. I even signed the envelope for you. It fit perfect in this envelope. I didn't want to bend it. So send me your ideas of this book thing and how much I can expect right from the start. I have a pathway for my funds set up already.

Write soon John. Let's talk turkey, so to say...

LATER MAN

Art

* * *

Hello John,

So far I have a little over 60,000 words completed. I have several poems and recipes added to the book. I will do a few more pages on my life in prison and what I had accomplished even though I still didn't DO THE RIGHT THING BY GOING STRAIGHT.

I am sending a letter to my wife telling her she can get a divorce if she wants one for not writing to me or even sending me her new phone number! I have written several letters and not one answer has come back nor have her kids answered my letters either!!! So they all get left out in the cold so to say. If my wife does not love me enough to even write or even let me call her she can sit in the cold too!!!

I have one very good lady friend who moved from near here to Florida and she does not like it down there much. She claims that the prices of everything are so damn high when it shouldn't be. What a fine looking sexy number she is too!!! This young woman has had a hard way to go. She will be given a spine operation soon. She can barely walk and has three kids to support. Her husband up and left her two years ago and moved to Atlanta, Georgia. He has since gone down and got his son to visit him in Georgia. I told her that he will be planning on doing just that and here is the proof of that statement! All fine and good until she asked for money him to help support the kids! Then he ups and leaves. Smart!

Man, it's getting cold around here now! The leaves are turning all different colors. Soon to be deer season. I know a few two-legged deer I'd like to get my hands on...hahahaha

John, when this goes through you and I will become brothers, thick as glue...SMILE

Do you have a phone or a cell phone? One of these days you can call my so-called wife because I can't reach her on a collect call.

I finished one recipe that I know you will like real good: EARTHWORM CHOCOLATE CHIP COOKIES: How does that sound to you John??? I've ate them and they are very chewy and tasty... hahahaha One will never know they are made with night crawlers until someone informs them of it... Every recipe that is in this book I have made and tried! I have a few paintings to mail out very soon.

LATER JOHN

It frustrated me to no end that Shawcross had no sense of how doomed our project was. I was eager to go ahead on everything, but he was rather stubborn about being more forthcoming with the manuscript, which I needed to get busy refining to get any sort of a deal. I had no problem drawing a contract up with Shawcross. It wouldn't have mattered, though, because the publisher wasn't going to offer any upfront money or make any promises until they had the manuscript in hand. I tried to explain it to the man, tried to double-emphasize the importance of sending the manuscript, particularly. But the bottom line was that he was impatient and so that was that.

The writing was literally on the wall by then. It was over.

JOHN:

I am very disappointed in what you have informed me of!!! If I give up the whole story, what is to stop anyone from running away with it and publishing it without a fucking dime? I figured you knew this but failed to inform me! Did you or didn't you?

WHAT DO I GET THAT WILL MAKE ME HAPPY IN GIVING UP THE WHOLE THING? You informed me of one thing, then without saying anything suddenly you go with someone else. I don't like shit like that John! I don't have the money to mail this whole package anyway! So the plans I had for the holidays went down the drain on a thought on your part. Now I am very much afraid of losing the whole thing and getting nothing! This guy you found wants the parts that are juicy only. If that is the case, just send back my twenty pages and we can forget about it. No one gives up everything! Something like this, a lawyer should be involved. You have not even drawn up a contract with me in any way, shape or form John. I was even told by you that was not a true statement. Something in your ball court is not right!

What happened to an advance? That you have to check on yourself or invest in the project yourself. And you don't have a dime either or so you have told me.

No Contract, No book: I won't have a leg to stand on. I have been burned many times before.

I feel something just is not up to par!

I am sorry John. We have got a lot to speak about because at this moment I don't feel safe in giving up the whole thing without something to show for it. People must think I have money when I am broke all the time. David Berkowitz has money up the ass it seems because he goes to the store and spends big bucks where I can only afford a book of stamps every two weeks!

NOW THIS PUPPY IS IN YOUR CORNER. I am not about to give up the whole manuscript without anything in writing and notarized!

I need a bidding contract of sorts that protect my investment.

Right at this moment I don't feel very well.

I am not pissed off just discouraged!!!

Art

"Something in your ball court is not right!"

No shit, Shawcross. But that's beside the point. Although he was not entirely mistaken on this accusation-- keep in mind, I was not exactly sober throughout most to all this--I was still on point as far as communication with the agent, who was talking with the publisher, which wasn't going well. But that wasn't my fault. Shawcross's own paranoia brought the project down. Now, I may have been struggling with numerous shades of my own madness, but I understood well what the publisher wanted and knew how to deal with the agent. After all, I was the one who secured the agent and made the project possible. Shawcross knew none of this, and the business side to this work seemed beyond his reasoning, although it does make sense that someone in prison for killing and eating numerous people might be affected by the occasional syntax error in his thought processes. It doesn't make it any less frustrating, though. So, with his refusal to send the rest of the book manuscript, we simply stopped having anything to do with each other and the partnership was ultimately dissolved. And we chose different devils to pursue.

CHAPTER ELEVEN

AMERICAN SON OF A BITCH

Luck and blessings have come to mind throughout the course of our relationship. Toward the end of this writing, I rediscovered a forgotten letter through some dark-handed serendipity. Shawcross had Scotch-taped a custom-made five-leaf clover and a four-leaf clover above the letter's heading. The curiosity recurs to me as to how we met. And why? I don't believe either of us needed our respective derangements reinforced. Nor could one really call it a "blessing," as such. The only reason I'd refer to our crossing paths in this manner is from a lesser of two evils standpoint. The same with my alcoholism. Had both not come into my life, the hopelessness and loneliness would've gotten to a place of pushing me to somehow finalize suicide. So, who is to say what a blessing really is? Maybe the universe just works with what it has.

7/17/02

JOHN

It is rare to find a five-leaf clover. You have FIVE WISHES now!

Regards for the ribbons. I used then ones I had that did not fit my machine--a bit loose but still it works.

I've not heard from Maria for a while now. That address I gave you, I hope she is there! I sure would like to rattle her bones & cat: meow: HAHA

What city does that gal you write to up in Maine live in? Only 150 miles. Man, I'll drive that far! My wife drives 5 ½ hours just to hug me and touch things. I also write to a hot sexy gal in Maine. She is WAXED! Got a mouthful pussy too! I got in a new one from New Zealand. A 42 year old HOUSEWIFE with two teenage children. Now why does she find ME attractive? Everyone wants a piece of ME. HAHA

Did you know, John, that a Jewish gal cannot get married with hair on her pussy?!

My 4th of July was one of sickness and shits! Bad food served here! A lot of people got the shit kicked out of them for real! HAHA Even the GUARDS. One of the civilian cooks got reamed over that! He might get fired!

Not a thing went on in the U.S.A. concerning the ragheads! So why tell people to beware?!

One more home was raided near here for over $40,000 worth of fireworks. Big Deal. Where is the spirit of Uncle Sam when its assholes raid you and kill the very idea of a celebration?!

No more will a plane be used to hit this country...

Bin Laden is DEAD!!!

Better close now brother. Take it easy.

Art

I finally got around to hanging myself in October of 2015.

Everyone who could've or would've helped me was passed on or simply gone. I was a man banned. Banned from people's lives, their homes, bars, liquor stores, and, for some reason, a gas station even though I've never owned a car. Shut out from seemingly everywhere. After initially being kicked out of the bunker, I was kept in the police station holding cell until the judge saw me that same afternoon and released me on personal recognizance. Then, still half-intoxicated and having bloodied my fists punching the inside of the police transport vehicle and the door of my jail cell, I dragged myself back to the bunker. I had nothing and needed clothing and other personal items. Plus, I still had a full drink I'd mixed right before the cops came to arrest and remove me. Before heading back, though, directly from the courthouse I zipped over to the same liquor store I was barred from and, not recognized for my infamy by some of the newer clerks there, picked up another half-gallon of Bacardi. While I was in line I bumped into an old temp agency acquaintance--a man of very questionable allegiances to the female gender, but never enough to be a nuisance to me (as too many males in my life have been). As might be expected, he was looking at me like I'd crawled off the stage of a live snuff performance. After all, I was sporting bloody, freshly-scabbed fists, just by-the-skin sober enough to be allowed to buy the bottle. Not drunk, but not yet ready to operate heavy machinery, and more disheveled than the effete, gnome-like man had seen after the many brutal jobs we'd been in the trenches on together (which was indeed an ugly state).

"Oh, hey," I remember casually greeting him. I was too elated at having been released to be as awkward or embarrassed as I should've been. "How's everything? Don't mind me, they just let me out of jail."

He was the one who seemed like he was in the wrong place at the wrong time, when he said rather simple-mindedly, which was the usual for him, "Jeez, I've never been to jail."

After bagging the rum, I immediately violated the restraining order Uncle Jerry had taken out only two hours before. I did attempt to reason with him after he heard me from upstairs in his apartment, entering what was my now former residence, as I had nowhere else to go. I was experiencing a complete disconnect from reality. I could hardly believe that the drink was still there, adding to the elation of release and far more interesting than having any pointless dialogue with this imbecile. I didn't think that he'd call the police again but he did, and they came in as I was sipping the drink just after taking off my pants, shoes, and socks. I was getting ready to go to sleep, oblivious to the supreme predicament I was in. So, I was arrested for the second time that afternoon! Who gets arrested twice in the same afternoon, within less than three hours?

One officer took hold of a wrist and I knew Hell itself was finally caving in on me. I wished that I got to finish the drink.

"Can you please get me a pair of pants and shoes or something?" I asked as politely as I could, although I was feeling betrayed on every side.

Amazingly, the cop putting the cuffs on me had some mercy or took pity. "He's a gentleman," he reassured his partner, "get him the pants over there and that pair of flip flops."

The other officer draped the pants over my shoulder and let me slip on the sandals, but I wasn't given the chance to put on the pants. Basically, I was escorted out to the front of house in the daylight in my boxer briefs. Though, it was all too stunning for me to care.

While I was being booked—for the second time that day--the officer who had asked the other cop to grab a pair of pants and something for my feet told me that, if it were up to him, he and his partner would drive me themselves to wherever I needed to go. It's only that restraining orders were taken so seriously that his own hands were tied. I understood there was nothing that could be done then but pray for the judge's continued goodwill.

That was a long, cold night. I ripped the t-shirt I was wearing trying to pull my body up into it like some childish rendition of a cocoon. Plus, further adding insult to misery, I had no socks on and my feet were freezing. They'd stay that way for several days in the Nashua Street Jail. And goddamnit, I had forgotten my eyeglasses. That meant I'd be nearly sightless until I had the police escort me back to the bunker in the hopes of the glasses still being there. I'd taken them off only moments before the sequel arrest and, in the confusion, forgot to ask for those. I would've easily traded the pants for the eyeglasses, as I'm almost legally blind without them! Even at the worst of the worst of detox meltdowns and everything else, I hadn't known what shit felt like until I was right up the cramped asshole of despair.

And again, no five hundred dollars produced from anywhere for bail. It is among the more deeply depressing, isolating experiences when your public defender is doing her sincere best to work with you at contacting family members to perhaps help with bail but, basically, everybody is either dead or broke, or dead broke, or they just simply don't care. So, off to county. That is, until the lawyer applied for the Massachusetts Bail Fund and I was released after ten days. If the bail had been above five hundred I would not have been let out. That's why the court officer had told me I was "lucky" as he was escorting me out of the courtroom to be further shackled for transport to Nashua Street. The judge, he tried reassuring me, could've set it so high that even if I were a billionaire it wouldn't have mattered. The district attorney, I recall, was asking for quite a bit more, of course, but the judge came back with, "I don't think Mr. Fay would be dumb enough to go back to the place again." Honestly, I wasn't so sure. That's how emotionally destroyed I was at the time. Although I was grateful the Honorable Judge McDonald had obviously taken pity on the torn and tattered little drunk.

In jail, so desperate to occupy time, I would find the books with the largest print and come close to bursting my eyes out of their sockets, madly squinting to read right up against the fluorescent light over the sink as I stood on a chair in the cell. When I first met my celly, I was in this odd stance and he later told me that he'd seen a lot of strange things while he was in jail but that was definitely the weirdest. Reading, however, is odd to people these days anyhow.

I was in the middle of getting the previously mentioned half haircut by an Islamic young man on the evening before my thirty-ninth birthday when one of the COs announced that I was getting bailed and to pack up everything in my cell. As if the grim comedy needed a cockroach-covered cherry on top, I had to leave and try to rebuild my life with half a shave and a haircut. Literally, only the left side of my face was shaved when I walked out of the jail that balmy August evening. And I would've had the same torn t-shirt I accidentally ripped up trying to keep warm at Station 7's jail had another newly-released inmate not had something of a heart and given me an intact shirt that he happened to have been arrested in. Fate is weird all right. And it hasn't gotten any less weird.

"What is a Section 35?"

"Section 35 is a Massachusetts law that allows a person to request a court order requiring someone to be civilly committed and be treated involuntarily for alcohol or drug abuse."

"What is civil commitment and who is it used for?"

Involuntary or civil commitment (also known as sectioning in some jurisdictions) is a legal process through which an individual who is deemed to have symptoms of severe mental disorder is court-ordered into treatment in a psychiatric hospital."

The very first night of my civil commitment to Bridgewater State Hospital under a Section 35, they locked me up in "the cell," their version of what is commonly referred to throughout the U.S. as "the hole." I was stripped down and wrapped up in a "monkey suit," as one of the corrections officers referred to it, to prevent suicide attempts and self-harm. The rest of the compound constituting MASAC (Massachusetts Alcohol & Substance Abuse Center) was a dormitory-style setting. I wasn't especially suicidal at the time, but, apparently, the threats reported by family members to set about severing their hands, heads, et al, were taken far too seriously and the staff needed time to take a closer look at me and evaluate my mental goings-on. It wasn't without merit; I was more insane than usual, which is bad. The following morning, an attractive blonde woman counselor whose head was shrinkable (and who was paradoxically key to the soonest possible discharge-- thirty days as opposed to the maximum of ninety) pulled a desk and chair up to opened door of the cell. It was quite a surreal setup, especially as I was standing in front of this woman naked except for the green, Velcro smock, which is a whole other level of first impressions. If I wasn't suicidal before, I was then. Although bizarrely turned on. Go figure. At least, it was the closest I had been to a woman seeing me without my clothes on for six years at that point. Of course, there was the nurse two years before who was nice enough to insert a catheter into my penis and urethra with all the mercy of a man-eating tiger who'd had a bad day. It wasn't love, but it was nicer than neglect. It's times like these when the association with Arthur Shawcross surfaces and I have to come up with something vaguely normal to try and explain it. We were working on his memoirs together, I told her, and had a business arrangement. Somehow, I forgot to mention my own cannibalistic intrigues. I also omitted the "friendly" strangulations, "Jeffrey Dahmer type" thoughts I'd been known to have had, drunken false imprisonments in the bunker. I even left out the cuff and shackle practice sessions. These lonely rehearsals did help, as I was complimented by the sheriff's deputy the night the transport van pulled up to the intake building on how "nimble" I was when hopping down out of the van onto the tarmac with the shackles around my ankles, without stumbling or getting tripped up. It was a peculiarly proud moment. The strip search was not as shining a moment (but they never are), a physical wreck after days of nonstop drinking and fist fighting with Dad (altercations he had initiated while intoxicated himself and running short on intelligent retorts).

And then, what's left? One may decide to sell his soul but the deeper question one has to ask: who's really buying and what are they going to do with it?

Shawcross died of cardiac arrest on November 10, 2008, cutting off any chance of reconciliation in this lifetime, which I would liked to have eventually attempted.

By then, I was more or less left mangled, mostly by my own hands, with the permanent scars to prove it. If you would like to come around and ask to see them sometime, let me know. Three-hundred-fifty Norco hydrocodones a month evened out with plenty of vodka for a party of one and ten personalities to feed; the pill bottles tucked under my blood-spotted pillow and the bottles under the covers like teddy bears; and a wake-up cocktail on the chair I used as a makeshift night table beside the bed. I bleed in my sleep. Some people talk in their sleep, I bleed in mine, as if blood runs out from my dreams. Particularly, during that period. But my health was not good. Although I was sincere in my occasional move to better myself, I was too far gone then. One of the most disappointing moments for me was when I tried to get back into martial arts training.

Kenny Florian was a UFC lightweight champion with whom I'd trained since his days at Boston Brazilian Jiu-jitsu. He and his brothers were starting their own school now and I was there on opening night. Even my sister and, most incongruously, my parents had come along. It was devastating for me when I couldn't last through the class. I was too physically sick and had to sit out most of that class.

It's true that the thoughts never seem to go away. Like recovering from alcoholism and other addictions, it's a day-by-day thing, or as one needs it, one tremor, one heart murmur at a time, if we're fortunate enough to still have a heartbeat at all.

Even I don't know everything that I've done, in the course of my own shit shows and general fuckery, until I read the victims' statements and police reports. It's more of a macabre set of circumstances than anything deliberately malicious. I feel like an exiled thing all out of fire here, where I never felt at home in this spiritually and geographically strip-mined wasteland.

Someday (one day, any day now) maybe my statement that the dead never die will make some sense to the mythic "sane" people (whatever hidden continent they might happen to reside on). The vision is mostly about distilling those objects of affection or derision down to the purity of their bones, boiled down to something fresh and virginal; a skewed admiration of intricate and delicate creations. One can love these things without fearing that they will be altered by time in a way that might cause substantial distress. Summing up, it's fair to state that the dead will never go away. In other words, a skeleton will probably be less apt to run off behind your back for a series of cross-country fuck-fests. So, really, it's security (Skeletal Security Insurance) and peace of mind for those with too many mental gremlin saboteurs to count. The dead will be the best and most loyal friends you'll ever have. Just academically noting, not necessarily condoning. Not necessarily.

A determined ghoul, though, can be quite resourceful. Grave robbing has come a long way, in that one doesn't have to rob graves anymore--or plunder crypts, bribe morticians, and kidnap coroners. It was always a dirty job, anyway, the passion of the old-school ghoul. You bring a skull home from the local cemetery, for instance, and suddenly your place is infested with mealworms and maggots. It's not a pretty sight, you will lose girlfriends, and the local police tend to lose their composure when they find that your spot is packed with human remains (or what they will later discover to be human remains as you try to figure out the most ingenious ways to kill yourself in your new suicide-proof cell). It's just not a practical option anymore. Or weirdest case scenario, your house ends up haunted with the ghost or ghosts of whoever's corpse you've tactlessly desecrated. Imagine you're sitting on the toilet one evening and a far-too-pale hand reaches up out of the water and rearranges your genitals in unpleasant ways.

It's no different with murder--maybe especially murder. Most people don't like to be murdered. Although, notably, that didn't seem to happen to Shawcross, the dead returning to make life difficult for the murderer. And I wondered about Dahmer's demons. Was Jeff just too drunk to notice the ghosts in Apartment 213?

The prospect, or at least the concept, of being haunted by somebody one had murdered has been a back-of-the-mind, backburner kind of deterrent for going that far with any of my alleged victims. As a researcher of the paranormal and practitioner of occult sciences and arts, I know there exist some pretty goddamn inexplicable things going on around us all. As for our physical faculties, we can only see and hear around one percent of our surroundings. Technically, your dead mother might be staring you right in the face and you wouldn't know it. Or reading this over your shoulder grinning like the Joker.

Part of me sometimes wonders if I was successful in the suicide, if my body is still out there in the woods of Wilmington, Massachusetts, hanging by the winter scarf that I tied with careful thoughtfulness around my neck, and if I'm dead as I write this account. In theory, it might explain a spooky thing or two: like when I upgraded my Android phone and only the numbers of those close to me who had died appeared under contacts. Incidentally, not everyone I know has passed away. Only most.

Regardless, either way, I proceed, dead or alive. I have to say, though, if I am deceased, my death has significantly improved my life. Case in point is this very book, which didn't surface, to provide hope and the most effective therapy I've ever had, until after the hanging. Just food for thought (and soberly wrenched from my soul--hence, the reason I used to take drugs).

Tending to split hairs when it comes to semantics and etymologies, my curiosity is ongoing as to whether I'm closer to being a human or a demon. Breaking it down to the simplest components, I tinker with esoteric etymology, according to which HU-MAN derives from HUE MAN, which refers to those kept as slaves. Although, looking into Black's Law Dictionary, the human being is defined as a "MONSTER." So, one may choose whichever direction that happens to suit him. However, "DE MON" is simply "THE MAN." Therefore, if I were to follow these lines of definition and depiction, I would rather prefer to think that I'm closer to "demon." If we are, in fact, in Hell, and 666 is the number of a man, then maybe all of us are demons. Then again, perhaps my ties to the kaleidoscope of shadows I've been inextricably and inexplicably connected to throughout life would point most people to the religious renderings of demons and fallen angels. Language aside, not many conventional men have, contemplating their home for decorative upgrades, earnestly thought to themselves, this place needs more skeletons. Of course, different shades and grades apply to everything and everyone. At the absolute least, at the darker end of the Yellow Brick Road, this is a story of recovery from suspected demon possession--or the delusion of possession--and the travesty of odysseys a mindset caught in this cycle takes one on.

Certain aspects of my own nightmare creation and dealings with Shawcross, truthfully, I don't want to remember, and normally I choose to distance myself. This might be a kind of guilt by dissociation. But I can't continue to lose sleep, ruin promising friendships, or harm myself. I'm forever profoundly affected by those wicked tides of the shadows and twilight; where worlds with walls of blood make sense. I don't know if I'm getting any better, and, as of this writing, may be getting worse. I just need to try to get on with my life after death.

(I WANT IT TO BE) THE END

AFTERWORD

One might ask why anyone would expose so much about his life. And I would say it's to shine such a glaring light on that which is meant to slither as undetected as possible in the darkness. For me, there wasn't a choice, other than to go a route which would've destroyed me and a lot of other people. In my own case, I'm grateful that I have writing as a means by which I can mitigate my issues. Being as saturated by corruption and general Devil-level madness as I am, this was definitely for the best.

Throughout my adult life, there has been a demon on one shoulder and a fed-up Christ on the other. The demon tempts and the Christ is so desperately tired of me he says, "Just do whatever you want, man." Picture a drunken Rodney Dangerfield as Jesus Christ…So, there is not a lot of breathing room to do the right thing—insofar as society is concerned anyway.

Add to all of that having had two fathers (bio-illogical and surrogate) who were both preternaturally brutal and separately taught me to kill, and there is a formula for something truly toxic. As much I disagreed with their views and cruelty, there were times when I found myself identifying with them and at least appreciating their training. And then, there was Shawcross. Arthur Shawcross, "The Monster of the Rivers" (etc.), was father number three.

It was a paternal trinity of death and destruction. At the time, Shawcross was the most sympathetic of the three. It never escaped me who he was or what he was convicted of but my bench was rather thin as far as friends or family. It was the best that I could do. Especially as I was cutting myself off from people in general. It was ideal to be invisible and have a very secret selection of connections. Truthfully, I became tired of having my personal monsters judged. I still don't always realize what a travesty they are until others point it out—usually, to the police. Worse, I lose potential friends or allies.

This book was a way of wringing out a soul oversaturated with devils; of re-directing hellish energies as a martial artist re-directs an opponent's attack. I'm not so delusional that I don't recognize the cancer of evil bringing shadows to every aspect of my existence. Therefore, the writing of it is my best therapy. See, I have yet to find the right counseling app that might offset the voices. In life, we work with what we have.

For More News About Brian Whitney
Signup For Our Newsletter:

http://wbp.bz/newsletter

Word-of-mouth is critical to an author's long-term success. If you appreciated this book please leave a review on the Amazon sales page:

http://wbp.bz/tsl

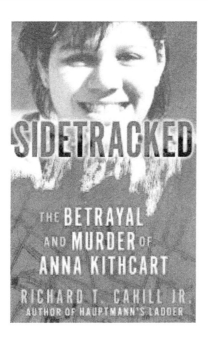

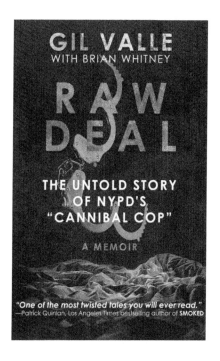

More True Crime You'll Love From WildBlue Press

BOGEYMAN: He Was Every Parent's Nightmare by Steve Jackson
"A master class in true crime reporting. He writes with both muscle and heart." (Gregg Olsen, New York Time bestselling author). A national true crime bestseller about the efforts of tenacious Texas lawmen to solve the cold case murders of three little girls and hold their killer accountable for his horrific crimes by New York Times bestselling author Steve Jackson. *"Absorbing and haunting!"* (Ron Franscell, national bestselling author and journalist)

wbp.bz/bogeyman

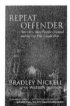

REPEAT OFFENDER by Bradley Nickell
"Best True Crime Book of 2015" (Suspense Magazine) A "Sin City" cop recounts his efforts to catch one of the most prolific criminals to ever walk the neon-lit streets of Las Vegas. *"If you like mayhem, madness, and suspense, Repeat Offender is the book to read."* (Aphrodite Jones, New York Times bestselling author)

wbp.bz/ro

DADDY'S LITTLE SECRET by Denise Wallace
"An engrossing true story." (John Ferak, bestselling author of Failure Of Justice, Body Of Proof, and Dixie's Last Stand) Daddy's Little Secret is the poignant true crime story about a daughter who, upon her father's murder, learns of his secret double-life. She had looked the other way about other hidden facets of his life - deadly secrets that could help his killer escape the death penalty, should she come forward.

wbp.bz/dls

BODY OF PROOF by John Ferak
"A superbly crafted tale of murder and mystery." – (Jim Hollock, author of award-winning BORN TO LOSE) When Jessica O'Grady, a tall, starry-eyed Omaha co-ed, disappeared in May 2006, leaving behind only a blood-stained mattress, her "Mr. Right," Christopher Edwards, became the suspect. Forensic evidence gathered by CSI stalwart Dave Kofoed, a man driven to solve high-profile murders, was used to convict Edwards. But was the evidence tainted? A true crime thriller written by bestselling author and award-winning journalist John Ferak.

wbp.bz/bop

Printed in Great Britain
by Amazon

20723960R00149